Let's Normalize Seeing Humanity First

Let's Normalize Seeing Humanity First

An Anti-Racist Guide for Working with Parents and Families in Schools

DANI PARKER MOORE

BLOOMSBURY ACADEMIC
NEW YORK • LONDON • OXFORD • NEW DELHI • SYDNEY

BLOOMSBURY ACADEMIC

Bloomsbury Publishing Inc, 1359 Broadway, New York, NY 10018, USA
Bloomsbury Publishing Plc, 50 Bedford Square, London, WC1B 3DP, UK
Bloomsbury Publishing Ireland, 29 Earlsfort Terrace, Dublin 2, D02 AY28, Ireland

BLOOMSBURY, BLOOMSBURY ACADEMIC and the Diana logo are trademarks of
Bloomsbury Publishing Plc

First published in the United States of America 2026

Copyright © Dani Parker Moore, 2026

For legal purposes the Acknowledgments on p. viii constitute an extension of this copyright page.

Cover image © iStock.com/PeopleImages

All rights reserved. No part of this publication may be: i) reproduced or transmitted in any form, electronic or mechanical, including photocopying, recording or by means of any information storage or retrieval system without prior permission in writing from the publishers; or ii) used or reproduced in any way for the training, development or operation of artificial intelligence (AI) technologies, including generative AI technologies. The rights holders expressly reserve this publication from the text and data mining exception as per Article 4(3) of the Digital Single Market Directive (EU) 2019/790.

Bloomsbury Publishing Inc does not have any control over, or responsibility for, any third-party websites referred to or in this book. All internet addresses given in this book were correct at the time of going to press. The author and publisher regret any inconvenience caused if addresses have changed or sites have ceased to exist, but can accept no responsibility for any such changes.

A catalog record for this book is available from the Library of Congress.

ISBN: HB: 978-1-4758-6509-7
PB: 978-1-4758-6510-3
ePDF: 979-8-7651-6098-5
eBook: 978-1-4758-6511-0

Typeset by Deanta Global Publishing Services, Chennai, India
Printed and bound in the United States of America

For product safety related questions contact productsafety@bloomsbury.com.

To find out more about our authors and books visit www.bloomsbury.com and
sign up for our newsletters.

This book is dedicated to Landon and Laiana. You two are my inspiration! May you be able to see a world where your full humanity is recognized!

Contents

Acknowledgments viii

Introduction 1

1 When Will It Be Over? 5

2 Are You Karen? 27

3 Doing the Work 49

4 Working with the People in Front of You 71

5 Get in Good Trouble 99

About the Author 115

Acknowledgments

To Landon and Laiana, I want you to know that I love you dearly! Enjoy reading! The world is limitless with the more you read and know!

To my husband, Donell. You have been on this journey with me since graduate school. You are my best friend and biggest cheerleader! When I am tired of writing, you hold me down. Thank you! Love you always!

To my friend Dr. Sherri Williams. Thank you for your friendship and encouragement. Thank you for pushing me the encouragement to write a book proposal and send it to Rowman & Littlefield (now Bloomsbury Academic). Without your belief in me, I would not be here. Thank you for the weekly writing meetings, laughter, and support.

To my birthday twin brother, Matt Williams. Your encouragement and steadfast support! It means the world to me. Thank you for always cheering me on!

To my mother-in-law, Freida Moore. You never stopped asking me about the book. You made me believe I needed to be on every stage sharing its message. Even when I was tired of writing, you kept pushing me! Thank you for always believing in me! You are truly missed.

To my mom and dad, Danita and Lionell Parker. Your encouragement and constant push to believe in the possibilities are greatly appreciated. Thank you for always believing in me.

To my sister Lauren, thank you sister for always lending an ear to listen and offering words of encouragement when I needed them most.

To my sister-in-love, Melody Moore, thank you for being the best sister in love anyone could ask for! Always encouraging and supporting me along the way!

To my mentor, coach, editor, and friend Dra. Aurora Chang, I would not be in this position without you! You were a calm voice amid the chaos of navigating the tenure process. A reassuring voice when I couldn't see the way. Your encouragement with our weekly check in kept me grounded. I'm thankful to have met you on this journey and can't thank you enough!

To the Wake Forest University Office of the Provost and Dean. Thank you for the generous support in funding my work. This book would not have been possible without your investment in my professional development. Your commitment has allowed me to grow as a scholar and produce work that centers humanity in meaningful ways.

To my editors at Rowman & Littlefield (now Bloomsbury Academic), Carlie Wall and April Snider—Thank you for giving me the opportunity to bring my vision to life in book form. Your patience, guidance, and belief in this project have been deeply appreciated.

Introduction

In the spring of 2020, as protests raged across the world amid the global pandemic, I sat holding my newborn daughter and asked myself a question that changed everything.
What will I say to my sweet Black children?
My husband and I had recently moved to Greensboro, North Carolina, settling into a racially mixed neighborhood, though our cul-de-sac was predominantly white. The world erupted in protests over the murders of George Floyd, Ahmaud Arbery, and Breonna Taylor. I found myself glued to the television, taking in the news, unable to look away.
I thought about my husband, a beautiful dark brown skinned man, who has also had an incident of racial injustice with a local law enforcement officer in his hometown. The officer wanted him to take his hat off, because the hat wasn't facing the correct direction. This interaction landed my husband in the local county jail. My husband, who was at the time a freshman in college home for the Thanksgiving holiday, was at a local party. This interaction was later dismissed, but none the less leaves an impression on him today. I thought about my high school friend—a brilliant Black doctor who posted his 5:30 a.m. runs daily, encouraging us all to stay active. I thought about me and my Black girlfriends, who like Breonna Taylor also lived in apartments where past tenants were still associated with our address. How a reminder of systemic disparities associated with no-knock warrants could happen to any of us in Black communities policed by overzealous officers shooting without looking. I have always been aware of the injustices Black Americans face due to white supremacy, but this time felt different, as the result of us watching everything unfold on national TV, this time it was met with global protest, corporate America deciding to say Black Lives Matter. It also felt different, as now I'm a mom of two little Black children for whom I must prepare them for this society and be constantly met with the fatigue of worry.
I watched as WNBA players took bold stands, inspiring a wave of activism across the sports world. I saw protests erupt across the globe. *This time had to be different, could we as a society truly make progress on racial injustice?*
I also thought of my students—the ones I have taught for nearly twenty years. Their names may not have made national headlines, but their lives and families have been shaped by these same

realities. And even if they haven't personally experienced these injustices, as Black Americans, they live with the ever-present fear that they might.

As I sat with these emotions—fear, anger, and determination—I knew I needed to do more than just reflect. I needed to act. That is why I wrote this book—for those who will work with students like mine, with families like mine. My hope is that, after reading it, you will be moved to recognize and honor the humanity of Black and Brown people in ways you may not have before.

Since I first began writing, much has changed in response to the uprisings of 2020. Laws have been passed restricting books, limiting what can be taught in classrooms, and even curtailing professional development topics. But despite these changes, one thing remains: *we must see the humanity in one another and make the conscious choice to be anti-racist.*

As you read this book, I ask you to remain open. See Black and Brown children as you see your own—full of potential, worthy of protection, and deserving of joy. See Black and Brown families as your neighbors, your friends, and your kin. And most importantly, see your own role in shaping a more just world. No action is too small.

Recently, I sat with my seventy-four-year-old aunt, who shared how her high school graduation was canceled when her all-Black school was shut down for desegregation. No school official told the students directly; they learned about it on TV. When they were forced into the white high school, they were met with daily violence and hostility. A few years later, my father attended that same school. One afternoon, he questioned why a white classmate was allowed to return to campus during open lunch while a Black student was arrested for the same action. For that question, my father was arrested.

These stories are not relics of the past. They shape our present. Seventy years after *Brown v. Board of Education*, our schools remain deeply segregated. Anti-Blackness still permeates our institutions.

I hope that as you read this book, you reflect on your role in this reality. More importantly, I hope you take away concrete practices that center the humanity of Black and Brown students and their families. I hope it helps you recognize how anti-Blackness shows up—and, more crucially, how to dismantle it.

It is not enough to acknowledge these realities. We must act. The future of our children—of our world—depends on it. Let's begin.

> Those who are racially marginalized are like the miner's canary: their distress is the first sign of a danger that threatens us all. It is easy enough to think that when we sacrifice this canary, the only harm is to communities of color. Yet others ignore problems that converge around racial minorities at their own peril, for these problems are symptoms warning us that we are all at risk.
>
> *(Guinier and Torres, 2003, p. 11)*

Goals for Reader:

- Develop a deeper understanding of racism in contemporary society and its systemic impact.
- Critically analyze the power of media and its influence on public perception and individual mindsets.
- Examine the long-term consequences of racism on individuals, communities, and institutions.
- Define and apply anti-racist pedagogy in educational and social contexts.
- Recognize how media portrayals of current events reflect and reinforce racial inequities in schools and society.

Introduction

For years, I've worked on this book, but it wasn't until a trip to Wilmington, North Carolina—a place rich with both personal history and the scars of racial injustice—that I fully understood its urgency.

Wilmington is the birthplace of my father and all of his siblings. As a child, I spent summers playing with my cousins and sitting on my grandmother's porch, soaking in the warmth of family and familiarity. Though my grandparents have since passed, I longed to reconnect with relatives I had not seen in years—delayed by the pandemic, then by the relentless demands of daily life.

My husband and I planned the trip as both a family getaway and an educational experience. My son, then six, could have an excused absence for our visits to the NC Aquarium and the *USS North Carolina* battleship. But for my kids, who were four and six at the time, the real highlights were the simple joys of the park and the beach.

We started our first day at the park where most of the kids appeared to be under the age of eight. The scene was pure and uncomplicated—kids of all races and socioeconomic statuses running freely, laughter filling the air. My son quickly made friends with other boys his age as they played a game of tag. My daughter, independent and confident, asked other parents to push her on the swing and various playground structures. I nervously watched her closely, my heart tugged by a quiet anxiety. How would these parents—strangers, mostly white—respond to my Black daughter's openness?

At one point, I ran over to help her after helping my son, to find her already being pushed by another mother—a white mother. I rushed over, instinctively ready to intervene, but before I could, she responded with "We're moms, we're here to help each other out." I was surprised by her response.

As my son played tag, a little boy ran straight into the round swing, busting his lip. He ran off in tears to find his mother. I followed, offering to help. His mother, flustered with an infant in a stroller, looked around for her husband—who had stepped away. Without hesitation, I handed her a napkin. "Thank you," she said, relief washing over her face.

She yelled to the dad for help. I told the mom what happened to her son, gave her some paper towels, and she thanked me multiple times. She, too, was a white mom. After helping him, I ran to find my daughter who was instructing another mom, a Black mom, to push her on yet another play structure. As I apologized to this mom, we struck up a conversation. She was a Black woman, recently relocated to the area from Connecticut, hoping to escape the bitter winters and the pressures of demanding family members.

Meanwhile, the playground was alive with joy. All of the children, regardless of race or class, ran freely, laughing, climbing, and swinging—just being. All of us parents were just watching our kids fully present, taking it all in. For that moment, time slowed. As parents, we all just wanted our kids to be happy and find joy, or perhaps we all wanted them to get tired out so we could go to bed early. Maybe we just wanted a moment of peace. Whatever the reason, there was a quiet, unspoken humanity there in all of us simply parenting our children.

The park could have been anywhere in America, but for me, it was Wilmington, North Carolina—a place tied to my childhood memories but also to the painful history my father often shared. Memories of racial segregation cast a shadow over the beaches, creating a lingering distance between my family and the shore. This trip, however, gave me the chance to learn a little more—to connect past and present in a way that felt deeply personal.

While I was there I made it a point to go visit my aunties, uncle, and cousins. Our first stop was to visit my dad's oldest sister, Angie. Aunt Angie is one of the sweetest people you could ever meet. I have fond memories of her visits. She has a way of ending her sentences with "Chile" and an infectious laugh. She was recently featured in the local *Wrightsville Beach Magazine* in an article entitled "Joy Realized: A Step in the Right Direction." The piece celebrated the long-overdue legacy graduation for the classes of 1969 and 1970. This was an attempt to celebrate for the people in those classes, because their school, Williston, closed abruptly when the school board voted to close it fourteen years later after *Brown v. Board of Education*.

As we sat and talked, I mentioned the magazine article, telling her I had seen it covered on the local news—she was so proud! She proceeded to pull out all of the newspaper articles and the very magazine I saw earlier. She described how one of her classmates reached out to everyone to ask if they would be interested in having a celebration graduation they had been denied. I proceeded to ask Aunt Angie, *how did you find out Williston was closing*? Here response stunned me, "We saw it on TV."

No warming. No formal announcement. No school official even had the decency to tell them their beloved school would be closed. To understand the magnitude of this, I looked further into this story. According to *Port City Daily*, Williston Senior High School was an all-Black high school that operated in the years 1954–68. During that time, my aunt describes attending a school full of pride and teachers that profoundly cared for their students. She described an award-winning marching band, and a chorus that brought home trophies year after year. It was more than a school—it was a place where students thrived, supported by educators who say their potential.

When the school board voted to close Williston, those students weren't just displaced—they were thrown into a hostile environment at predominantly white schools. Aunt Angie recalled the constant fights, the resentment from white students who didn't want them there, and the loss of Black teachers who had once been their mentors.

Then she asked me, "Have you heard of the Wilmington Ten?"

I nodded.

She leaned in, "They were my friends."

She told me how, as a young girl, she participated in a march to protest Dr. Martin Luther King Jr.'s assassination. My grandmother, weary of what Black folks endured in the South, feared for her safety. Some marches, Aunt Angie recalled, were quickly dispersed by police.

Then, there was my father whom she called the "militant" one. He was arrested after asking why white students are allowed to return from lunch late and Black students were punished for doing so. He spoke up, and for that, he was arrested.

The lived experience of Black folks living in Wilmington, North Carolina, is complicated. Young people were forced to navigate racism daily—whether in classrooms, their neighborhoods, or the streets they walked. The delayed desegregation of schools, the criminalization of Black youth, and the trauma endured by my Aunt Angie, my dad, and the Wilmington Ten illustrate a painful truth: racism is pervasive and traumatic and, if we are not intentional in the pursuit for justice, we will continue to find ourselves trapped in this cycle.

Even today, young people in North Carolina face systemic inequities in education. While there is no federal constitutional right to education, North Carolina's constitution states in Article I, Section 15, "The people have a right to the privilege of education, and it is the duty of the State to guard and maintain that right." Therefore, in a state where it is the people's right to education and it's the state's duty to maintain that right, every student deserves to be seen, valued, and treated with respect and humanity.

What strikes me most about my family's experience is how deeply their education was shaped by discrimination and racism—particularly during the years of 1968–1972. Many of the stories my father shared from his childhood revolved around moments of the most traumatic forms of racism and systemic injustice. These stores included cross burnings, arrests, and targeted violence from strangers, all designed to intimidate and suppress Black communities. Yet, despite enduring some of the most traumatic forms of racism imaginable, my father remained steadfast in his belief in education. His advocacy for learning became his form of resistance, outweighing even the most vicious attempts to silence him.

Throughout my youth, I absorbed these stories, often paired with warnings—cautionary lessons about the ill intent of white people in power. My father graduated from high school in 1972, and I was born in 1981—just nine years later. Though I was raised in what was considered the post-civil rights era, the trauma inflicted upon Black communities, particularly in schools, remained deeply embedded and far-reaching. The impact of those experiences didn't end with my father and aunt—it shaped the way they moved through the world, the way they raised their children, and the opportunities that were available to us.

As a Black woman in my forties, I belong to the generation that was taught we benefited from the Civil Rights Movement. We were led to believe that integrating schools with white students meant we did not have to endure the traumas our parents and grandparents faced. I, too, once believed the world would be different for my two kids.

As I have worked on this book, years have passed. I have witnessed both the joy and laughter of playing in the park with kids that are different from my kids, only to be met with the horror of seeing many of the outcomes of the Civil Rights Movement being undone. School boards are actively discouraging the use of diverse books, and recent reports from the Civil Right Project and researchers at North Carolina State University reveal a troubling truth: seventy years after *Brown v. Board of Education*, North Carolina, once regarded as a leader in desegregation efforts, now finds itself with increasingly segregated schools. Despite an increase in diversity among students, segregation patterns have worsened, with children from different racial backgrounds disproportionately grouped in schools with peers of the same race.

By 2021, Black students had the least interaction with white students, with the average Black student attending a school where only 28.3 percent of their peers were white (*New CRP Report Shows North Carolina Schools Losing Hard-Earned Progress on Integration—the Civil Rights Project at UCLA*, 2024). As a mother of two Black children, I am deeply concerned about the path we are on. The intentional dismantling of desegregation efforts from the 1980s and 1990s in North Carolina threatens to expose them—and their peers—to the same racial traumas that previous generations fought to overcome. According to the same report, from 1989 to 2021, North Carolina's public-school enrollment surged by over 41 percent and experienced a growing diversity. By 2021, the enrollment composition stood at 45 percent white, 25 percent Black, 20 percent Hispanic, 5 percent Multiracial, 4 percent Asian, and 1 percent American Indian and by 2021 Black students had the least exposure to white students.

As Guinier and Torres (2002) note, "Yet others ignore problems that converge around racial minorities at their own peril, for these problems are symptoms warning us that we are all at risk" (p. 11). We are at risk. Racism is not a relic of the past—it is a present and persistent reality. We must actively choose a different path. It takes all of us who care about education and students and their families to commit to anti-racist practices and center the humanity of students. We have to remember these stories are connected to real lives and have long-term effects on students and their families.

This chapter explores the power of stories—particularly those of young people. These are the stories we see in news cycles, yet their impact extends far beyond headlines. Like the experiences of my aunt and father, these stories carry weight, shaping the lives of students who come into our classrooms every day. The racial injustices we witness daily in the news feeds are not distant or isolated; they are deeply intertwined with the lived realities of our students and their families. Many of these issues have long been the focus of social justice advocates, but in recent years, the world has been forced to confront them in ways that can no longer be ignored.

This chapter will help readers understand that racism is not just an occasional tragedy highlighted on our screens—it is a persistent reality reflected in the everyday experiences of our students and their communities. The way we function as a society is mirrored in our classrooms, and we must recognize that the injustices we see in the media are the same ones shaping the lives of those we teach.

The national conversation around race relations have been particularly prominent over the last several years, driven by the rise in racial violence and systemic injustices disproportionately affecting people of color. More recently, elected officials have pushed policies aimed at banning Critical Race Theory in classrooms, banning books, and eliminating the African American AP Course in Florida. This turbulence has only grown, especially in light of the Covid-19 pandemic, which disrupted American life with a mandatory shutdown in March 2020. During this time, as millions were confined to their homes, the reality of racial injustice becomes inescapable. The 24-hour news cycle and the constant access to handheld devices created a culture of constant information being displayed to us at any moment.

While it is easy to become desensitized to this constant bombardment of information, educators and those working for students and families of color must understand that the choice to detach is not easy for people of color as it is a constant reminder of the racism we face and could face at any moment. To counter this, educators must make a deliberate choice: to reject complacency and embrace an anti-racist pedagogical approach. This book will not only help you reflect on this challenge but also provide strategies for foster inclusive, justice-centered learning spaces.

Between 2020 and 2023, several national cases reignited the national conversation about race relations in America, serving as a stark reminder of what DuBois posed over a century ago: "how does it feel to be a problem?" DuBois stated:

> Between me and the other world there is ever an unasked question: unasked by some through feelings of delicacy; by others through the difficulty of rightly framing it. All, nevertheless, flutter round it. They approach me in a half-hesitant sort of way, eye me curiously or compassionately, and then, instead of saying directly. How does it feel to be a problem? they say, I know an excellent colored man in my town; or I fought at Mechanicsville; or. Do not these Southern outrages make your blood boil? At these I smile, or am interested, or reduce the boiling to a

simmer, as the occasion may require. To the real question. How does it feel to be a problem? I answer seldom a word. (DuBois, 2015)

Several national cases occurred that prompted national outrage.

On February 23, 2020, twenty-five-year-old Ahmaud Arbery was out for a job in his neighborhood Satilla Shores, Georgia, when three white men, claiming to make a citizen's arrest, ended with Mr. Arbery shot and killed. The suspects spent nearly two months free as the local district attorney refused to press charges. It was not until the case made national news on May 5, 2020, through a leaked video of the full incident that there was an arrest on May 7, 2020. This racially motivated attack on Mr. Arbery was weeks before the May 25, 2020, incident in which Mr. George Floyd was killed.

The world erupted in protest following the video-recorded killing of Mr. George Floyd. The police were called to the scene of a local grocery store in Minneapolis, Minnesota, where the shopkeeper believed Mr. Floyd presented him with counterfeit money. Darnella Frazier, a seventeen-year-old bystander, captured the now-infamous footage. In the video, you can see a police officer kneeling on the neck of Mr. Floyd, as Mr. Floyd continues to attempt to share his inability to breathe. The bystander records the entire interaction, including seeing several people attempting to request the officer to remove his knee from his neck. Two other officers stood by without making any attempt to correct their colleague.

This on-camera death prompted national and international protests understanding the police brutality of Black people. While these cases garnered national attention, many were critical of the fact that Breonna Taylor's story was missing from the national headlines. In the summer of 2020, a national cry on social media brought attention to her case with tweets saying, "Arrest the cops who killed Breonna Taylor." Breonna Taylor was a twenty-six-year-old Black woman who was in her home with her boyfriend, when the police arrived to serve a no-knock warrant arrest. After no warning, the police began to shoot into the home, killing Breonna.

It wasn't until the #SayHerName movement and social media activism—including the viral demand to "Arrest the cops who killed Breonna Taylor"—that national attention turned to her case. The WNBA played a pivotal role in amplifying her story. Players used their platform to demand justice, wearing T-shirts with her name and placing her name on the gym floor during televised games. While these cases sparked global conversations, they also underscored the ongoing disparities in media coverage and justice for Black victims of police violence. The racial consciousness that surged in 2020 did not fade—it continues to shape the fight for accountability and systemic change.

While the racial injustices of spring 2020 may have seemed like a sudden surge, they were part of a long-standing pattern—a trend that has persisted for decades. As a nation, we have witnessed racialized conflicts repeatedly reported in the media. Many of these cases that are reported are often debated and moved on to the next sensational story. One such moment occurred in August of 2017, when the Unite the Right Rally was held in Charlottesville, Virginia. The rally consisted of members of the far-right groups including *right*, neo-Confederates, neo-fascists, white nationalists, neo-Nazis, and Klansmen. The groups walked across the campus of the University of Virginia chanting "We will not be replaced." In fact, one member of the rally rammed his car into a group of counter protesters, killing one and injuring several others. This rally was in direct response to the movement to remove several Confederate monuments across the country after the killing of several church members in Charleston, South Carolina, by a young white male, neo-Nazi, white supremacist. The push to dismantle Confederate symbols has existed for decades but has escalated in recent years, underscoring the ongoing struggle over how the nation reckons with its history of racism.

More recently, we have seen a movement across the United States in many local elections of 2022 to prevent Critical Race Theory from being taught in K-12 public schools to banning books that focus on diversity related to race. According to the American Library Association (ALA), a national poll indicated the following:

> Majorities of public-school parents affirm that various types of books should be available in school libraries on an age-appropriate basis. This includes works about U.S. History that focus on the role of slavery and racism in shaping America today, such as the "1619 Project" (84%); works of literature that use racial slurs, such as "Huckleberry Finn," "To Kill a Mockingbird," and "Of Mice and Men" (82%); novels for young adults that portray police violence against Black people, such as "Ghost Boys" and "The Hate U Give" (68%); fiction and non-fiction books about lesbian,

gay, and transgender individuals, such as "George" and "This Day in June" (65%); and works of fiction that have sexually explicit content, including scenes of sexual violence, such as "Beloved" and "Looking for Alaska" (57%). (Hlywak, 2022)

The Impact of News Cycles on Students

The racialized events we see in the news and popular culture are not isolated events that we can easily forget about. They are directly related to our students and their families. Even if your students do not live in Charlottesville, Virginia; Chapel Hill, North Carolina; or San Francisco, California, these incidents are happening across the country, reflecting the reality that our nation has yet to fully reckon with its legacy of white supremacy, Jim Crow laws, Japanese Internment Camps, English-only policies, and historical misinformation in our nation's textbooks and schools.

Professor Nora Gross has examined how Black youth navigate double consciousness through social media, particularly in their use of popular hashtags (Gross, 2017). One example is #IfTheyGunnedMeDown, a hashtag that highlights the racialized ways Black bodies are perceived through the white gaze. Gross's analysis of Instagram posts using this hashtag reveals a common pattern: Black teenagers often shared juxtaposed images—one casual as compared to a professional photo of them in graduation attire, military attire, and the like. Gross suggests the "double consciousness" of the young Black teens as an act in which they have to navigate respectability politics.

Similarly, the work of Professor Sherri Williams (2021) explores the psychological impact of witnessing police brutality against Black people, particularly Black women. Williams applies *Cultivation Theory*, which suggests that people who are frequently exposed to violence against Black bodies—begin to see those representations as reflective of social reality. Originally coined by George Gerbner (1998), Cultivation Theory argues that television and mass media shape the way audiences understand the world around them.

Williams extends this framework to social media, demonstrating how the constant circulation of racial trauma—such as viral videos of police violence—reinforces historical trauma for Black communities, especially Black women. Recognizing this ongoing exposure to trauma is essential. If we acknowledge its profound impact, we can be better equipped to support Black youth and Black women within institutions, communities, and social spaces that shape their lives.

As educators, we must constantly remind ourselves that racism exists, we are socialized to participate in it, and we must actively push against subscribing to it. The rise of "EdScare" (Friedman, 2022) is a clear example of this struggle. Republican leaders across the nation have weaponized fear, misleading parents into believing that schools are indoctrinating children with discussions about Critical Race Theory and issues related to LGBTQ identity. The daily news cycle of unjust and racialized and homophobic experiences cannot be dismissed as something happening in faraway places, nor can we assume someone else will address it. The harsh reality is that these incidents happen, and while they may not make our local news, they are reminders of the society in which we live.

Furthermore, we must understand that when these events hit our news channels or social media outlets, they are warnings to those who look like the victims. People of color are terrorized and in response often raise their children in ways that teach them how to navigate these harsh realities. Black children are often taught to be hypervigilant in their interactions with police and authority figures. Asian Americans remain keenly aware of their surroundings, fearing they may become victims of the next hate crime. When students walk into our classrooms each day, they bring these fears with them.

I remember when I was working in 2013 in Durham, North Carolina, at a summer program called Freedom School, one of my second graders shared that he was scared that someone would shoot him like Trayvon Martin. As a second-grade Black boy he was aware of what was happening in the news around Trayvon Martin's killer. That summer, the debate around "castle doctrine" and whether Trayvon Martin's killer had acted in self-defense. This national case underscored the injustice of a Black teenager simply walking through his own neighborhood, only to be racially profiled and killed.

While we often imagine these cases as discussions for adults, the reality is that they deeply affect young people. For Black youth, national tragedies feel personal—a reminder that their innocence, safety, and humanity are not guaranteed. We saw this again in April 2023, when sixteen-year-old Ralph Yarl was shot twice by an eighty-four-year-old white man simply for ringing the wrong doorbell while trying to pick up his younger brothers (AP, 2023). These cases are not exceptions—they are patterns. They are not distant stories—they are lived realities for our students. As educators, we must recognize, address, and challenge these realities in our classrooms.

While these stories dominate the news cycle, we must not become so desensitized that we forget the humanity of the students we serve. They see themselves reflected in the stories and the pain of hearing these stories or seeing them replayed on social media takes a toll on their psyche. Educators must see them as human beings that are not living separate lives that stop at the school doors. These news cycles should remind us that we as educators should provide space to allow our students to express themselves, share their stories, and view them with full humanity. When we approach our teaching with humanity, we see our students as we see ourselves and we recognize they are experiencing life just as we are. We teach our students with compassion, kindness, and belonging.

This framework allows us to recognize when our students and families see and experience racialized traumatic events, that these experiences take away from their humanity. In many schools, these very acts of injustice are replicated:

- We see cases of school resource officers being extra violent with Black girls, slamming them to the ground. In South Carolina, a Black girl was pulled and slammed to the ground when she would not put her cell phone up.

- In December 2021, a Black mother brought a lawsuit against the Lorain City Schools for the emotional distress brought to her by her nine-year-old Black daughter. The school district released a video of the girl being forced to eat food from a trash can by two white employees. The incident, caught on video, showed other children freely discarding food, yet a white cafeteria worker singled out the Black girl, made her wipe off the food with a paper towel, and forced her to eat it—while the white principal stood by and did nothing.

- In Chicago, IL, after a Black mother informed the school that she would be running late by ten minutes to pick up her child. Instead of understanding, the school administration called social services on her.
- During the pandemic, when schools transitioned to online instruction, a Black student was struggling to keep up with the work. A parent asked the teacher for a Zoom conference call. The teacher forgot to mute their microphone and launched into a racialized tirade, exposing deep-seated biases.

These are not isolated incidents—they are manifestations of the same systemic issues we see in the news. Over the last several years, as racial injustices have been increasingly exposed, opposition to racial progress has grown, giving rise to what is now called the "anti-woke" movement—a reactionary effort to suppress discussions of race, history, and justice in schools and society.

The goal of this chapter is to encourage you to reflect on how news and social media portray people of color and to consider how those stories impact your students and their families. How do these narratives shape the lives of the students in your classroom? Do they mirror the lived realities of your students? Do you have a plan to create space for students to process the events they see unfolding around them? In this chapter, we will also explore what it means to be anti-racist. This will be the groundwork and as we move through the book, you will see how adopting an anti-racist approach leads to better outcomes for all students. In addition, anti-racist pedagogy allows for better connections with families and parents.

Understanding the Complexity of Racism

The events I have outlined for you are rooted in racism, and racism is everywhere in our society. According to the American Psychological Association, racism is defined as:

> *n.* a form of *prejudice* that assumes that the members of racial categories have distinctive characteristics and that these differences result in some racial groups being inferior to others. Racism generally includes negative

emotional reactions to members of the group, acceptance of *negative stereotypes*, and *racial discrimination* against individuals; in some cases it leads to violence. (Retrieved from www.https://dictionary.apa.org/)

Scholars have helped us understand how racism functions in our society and how its systems are at play. Professor Bonilla-Silva (2022) writes that the common sense view attributes racism to bad individuals ("the racist"), which limits our capacity to understand its collective nature. Racism, in the mind of most people in the world, is a matter of a few rotten apples. In contrast, he argues that racism is the product of racial domination projects (e.g., colonialism, slavery, and labor migration). He suggests that once these racialized concepts entered our human history, racism became *embedded* in society, thus becoming systemic racism; racism becomes the *apple tree* (or central to the tree) rather than the rotten apples.

Using Bonilla-Silva's framework for understanding systemic racism, we must recognize that news stories rooted in racism are not isolated incidents or the result of a few bad actors. Instead, they reflect what Guinier and Torres (2002) describes as "problems are symptoms warning us that we are all at risk" (p. 11). Each of these national headlines illustrates how racism operates in society, and schools are not exempt from its impact. These systemic issues do not remain confined to the news cycle—they manifest in everyday interactions students experience, shaping their interactions both inside and outside of school settings.

Listening to Lived Experiences

Alvarez and Milner (2018) found that white teachers often reject discussions of racism, largely due to fear—fear of saying the wrong thing, fear of discomfort, or fear of backlash. Many teachers believe they are unprepared to engage in race talk and need skills to navigate these difficult conversations. As an educator, ask yourself: What is the fear *really* about? I often work with white teachers who express deep discomfort when discussing or teaching about race. Yet, I have also worked with white teachers who push past that discomfort, recognizing that the humanity of their students is far more important than their own temporary unease.

One afternoon in a hair salon, I listened as a Black mother, a salon owner, shared an experience at her daughter's school—one that left her angry, confused, and deeply hurt. She proudly described herself as an active volunteer, always purchasing supplies for her child's teacher, regularly communicating through the classroom app, and even chaperoning field trips. Her daughter's grandmother was also deeply involved in supporting her education. Yet, despite this strong partnership with the school, her first-grade daughter was denied permission to use the restroom during state testing. The young white teacher refused to let her go, and given the child's age, she was unable to hold it. She soiled her clothes in class.

What made this situation even worse was that the teacher never contacted the mother—even though she routinely used the classroom app to communicate. Instead, she sent a message to the grandmother, who was not as familiar with the technology, delaying any response. By the time the grandmother saw the message, the little girl had been sitting in her soiled clothes for an extended period. Outraged, the mother went to school administrators seeking answers: *Why was my child forced to sit in humiliation?*; *Why wasn't I contacted immediately?*; *Why wasn't basic compassion extended to my daughter?* However, instead of receiving empathy or accountability, the school responded by punishing the mother—revoking her permission to volunteer on field trips.

Unfortunately, this is not an isolated incident. Black women are frequently labeled as aggressive or difficult when they advocate for their children. This perception—rooted in racial bias—shapes how teachers, school administrators, and program leaders respond to Black mothers. Being a reflexive, equity-minded educator means asking:

- Would I have reacted the same way if this had been a white child?
- Would I have made a different decision if this were a white mother?
- Was there really no other option but to deny a six-year-old access to the restroom?

The heart of the issue is that the teacher chose not to call the mother directly—someone she regularly communicated with for less urgent matters. The message this sent was clear: Your child's discomfort is not a priority. Your role as an involved parent does not matter to us.

This experience echoes the recurring themes in my research on Covid-19 and Black mothers. Many shared that during online learning, they were not informed about their children's progress. They didn't find out about missing assignments or academic struggles until grades were already entered—by then, it was too late to intervene.

Challenging the Status Quo with Anti-Racist Practices

The opposite of racist isn't "not racist." It is "anti-racist." What's the difference? One endorses either the idea of a racial hierarchy as a racist, or racial equality as an anti-racist. One either believes problems are rooted in groups of people, as a racist, or locates the roots of problems in power and policies, as an anti-racist. One either allows racial inequities to persevere, as a racist, or confronts racial inequities, as an anti-racist. There is no in-between safe space of "not racist."
—Ibram X. Kendi, How to Be an Antiracist

In many circumstances, we must understand where we are in our own biases and prejudices. It's something that we have to notice, reflect, and pivot. While you may have only grown up in spaces that are homogeneous, the reality is that our classrooms, schools, afterschool programs, and summer programs are becoming more and more diverse. It is our responsibility as educators to change the status quo and provide an atmosphere that allows students to thrive and live to their fullest potential.

The inequities we encounter in educational settings are deeply emphasized by larger systemic forces. These power dynamics shape which school students attend, their access to community resources, and the ways they are disciplined. The communities in which students and their families live are often shaped by long-standing systems of oppression, with decades-long effects on educational opportunities. However, as educators, we have the power to disrupt these oppressive structures daily.

Let me share an example. I have a friend we will call Ms. Shirly. She is a dedicated community leader who runs an afterschool program for students attending a Title 1 middle school. She loves running this program. She operates it out of a local church fellowship hall, where students arrive by bus after school. As an afterschool program leader, Ms. Shirly advocates fiercely for her students—not just in her program, but also within their schools. When students struggle with teachers and administrators, she steps in to work with both families and school staff, ensuring that students receive fair treatment.

She is keenly aware of the long history of inequities in school discipline policies—policies that disproportionately impact students of color. Using her deep understanding of her students' lived experiences, she serves as a bridge between them and the school system, advocating for equity in how they are treated, disciplined, and supported.

Teachers have the power to shape how students are perceived and treated in their classrooms. When we think of school suspensions, the process often begins with a classroom, write up. In many schools, Black and Brown students are disproportionately disciplined compared to their white peers, with these disparities starting as early as Kindergarten.

Educators should be proactive in de-escalating situations before they become power struggles. Instead of reacting immediately, pause and reflect:

- Are you expecting the student to respond in a way that is stereotypical?
- Have you asked the student what might be happening outside this moment?
- Could there be external factors influencing their behavior?

A little curiosity and investigation can go a long way in preventing unnecessary discipline.

Recognizing we are all human and just as we have bad moments and days, so do our students. I often do an exercise with my students, asking them: *How does your body respond when you're hungry?* They often respond with headaches, lack of concentration, and stomach pains. I then remind them: The students they work with experience the same feelings, but with fewer options to address them. While some students may go to a campus cafeteria stocked with a variety of food choices—salad bars, grilled foods, smoothies, pizza, and health options. Others may not have that privilege. Something as simple as recognizing the feeling of hunger should remind us that while students may have similar needs, they often have less autonomy, fewer resources, or limited communication abilities to express them. As educators, our role is to approach students with empathy and awareness—not just as learners, but as individuals navigating complex realities both inside and outside the classroom.

Conclusion

This chapter has highlighted key experiences of my family and students, illustrating the deep human connections we all share. While systematic oppression remains a reality, it does not have to be the norm. We must make a deliberate choice to center humanity in the spaces where we work with youth. The relentless news cycle of oppression and racism serves as a reminder that these are not isolated incidents. For many students, these news stories mirror the realities of their own communities. To disrupt these patterns, we must commit daily to creating spaces of empathy, understanding, and social justice—where all students feel seen, valued, and supported.

Reflection Questions

1. What are the stories you have learned from your family about their school experiences? How did school impact them? Were you warned about certain groups of people, and if so, how did those stories shape your perspective?

2. What is your own school story? Reflect on the teachers who shaped you—did you have teachers of color? Friends of color? How did those relationships influence your understanding of race and education?
3. What are the school experiences of the young people you work with? How do their stories reflect the larger realities of race and education in your community?
4. Many communities of color have faced racism and trauma in school settings. This type of trauma often shapes how students and families feel about school and community spaces. When building relationships with students and families, how do you acknowledge and address these realities?
5. Considering national and local news cycles, how do you respond to racialized experiences when you hear about them? What are your immediate thoughts and how do you process them?
6. When a national news story affects people of color, do you create space for your students to process their feelings in class? What would that look like in your subject area? For example, could students write an essay about their emotions and then discuss in small groups?
7. When significant events happen in the news, how can you collaborate with your colleagues to debrief and determine the best ways to support your students?
8. When your community shares experiences of racial injustice, how do you respond? Do you listen and advocate for change, or do dismiss it as an isolated incident? How can you actively support those affected?

Action Steps

1. At the start of your programming year, take time to assess the students you are serving. Ask them about their interests, what brings them joy, and their personal goals for the year.

2. Engage with the families to learn about their cultural values, traditions, and any important aspects of their background that could help you better support their children?
3. Research your local and state's demographics for your student population. What were the key trends in the previous school year? How are students performing? Look beyond the online data—what gaps exist in the information? How can you build a fuller picture of student needs?
4. As you plan programming for the school year, how can you incorporate the values, interests, and goals of your students and families? Do the materials in your space reflect the students you serve? Can you involve families and community members as mentors, guest speakers, or workshop leaders?

References

AP. (2023, April 19). *What We Know So Far about the Shooting of Kansas City Teen Ralph Yarl.* AP News. https://apnews.com/article/ralph-yarl-shooting-kansas-city-black-teen-154c4e3275732b83bc9f0026a9981b81.

Alvarez, A., and Milner IV, H. R. (2018). "Exploring Teachers' Beliefs and Feelings about Race and Police Violence." *Teaching Education,* 29(4), 383–394.

Bonilla-Silva, E. (2022). "What Makes Systemic Racism Systemic?" In *Theories of Race and Racism: A Reader,* Third Edition (pp. 829–845). https://doi.org/10.4324/9781003276630-62

Civil Rights Project at UCLA, the. (2024). *New CRP Report shows North Carolina Schools Losing Hard-earned Progress on Integration.* https://www.civilrightsproject.ucla.edu/news/press-releases/press-releases-2024/new-crp-report-shows-north-carolina-schools-losing-hard-earned-progress-on-integration.

Du Bois, W. E. B. (2015). *The Souls of Black Folk.* Yale University Press.

Friedman, J. (2022, February 23). "Higher Ed Must Act Against Educational Gag Orders (opinion)." *Inside Higher Ed.* https://www.insidehighered.com/views/2022/02/24/higher-ed-must-act-against-educational-gag-orders-opinion.

Gerbner, G. (1998). "Cultivation Analysis: An Overview." *Mass Communication and Society,* 1(3–4), 175–194.

Gross, N. (2017). "#IfTheyGunnedMeDown: The Double Consciousness of Black Youth in Response to Oppressive Media." *Souls: A Critical Journal of*

Black Politics, Culture, and Society, 19(4), 416–37. https://doi.org/10.1080/10999949.2018.1441587.

Guinier, L., and G. Torres (2002). *The Miner's Canary: Enlisting Race, Resisting Power, Transforming Democracy*. Harvard University Press.

Hlywak, S. (2022, March 24). "Large Majorities of Voters Oppose Book Bans and Have Confidence in Libraries." *American Library Association*. https://www.ala.org/news/press-releases/2022/03/large-majorities-voters-oppose-book-bans-and-have-confidence-libraries.

Williams, S. (2021). Stream of sadness: Young black women's racial trauma, police brutality and social media. *Feminist Media Studies*, *21*(8), 1270–1284.

All our silences in the face of racist assault are acts of complicity.
— bell hooks, *Killing Rage: Ending Racism*

Goals

- Define the term "Karen" and its cultural and social implications.
- Examine highly publicized incidents where "Karen" behaviors have been documented.
- Analyze how Karen-like behaviors manifest in schooling contexts and their impact on students, families, and educators.
- Reflect on personal biases and behaviors to prevent contributing to Karening in educational or professional spaces.

Introduction

The term "Karen" has evolved beyond its original use, with the *New York Times* describing it as follows:

> Karen is no longer an easy name. Once popular for girls born in the 1960s, it then became a pseudonym for a middle-aged busybody with a blond choppy bob who asks to speak to the manager. Now, the moniker has most recently morphed into a symbol of racism and white privilege. (*New York Times*, 2020)

This chapter explores the cultural and systemic implications of the "Karen" phenomenon, focusing on how these behaviors manifest within school systems. Publicized incidents such as *Oakland Cookout Karen, Bird Watching Karen, Cellphone Karen in NYC, College Karen at Yale, Black Lives Matter*, and *Sidewalk Karen and Ken* illustrate the broader societal patter of white individuals weaponizing their privilege to police Black and Brown people's existence. However, these behaviors are not confined to viral videos—they are replicated in schools every day.

Educators and administrators who exhibit "Karen and Ken" behaviors often perpetuate harm on Black and Brown families by:

- Calling the police on students or parents where no crime has been committed.
- Reporting families to social services for minor infractions, such as being a few minutes late to pick up a child.
- Over-disciplining Black and Brown students for behaviors that would be overlooked in their white peers.

This chapter will examine real school-based incidents, such as:

- A white principal in Chicago who called DSS on parents for being five minutes late to pick up their child.
- A California teacher on Zoom who unknowingly recorded herself expressing disdain for Black parents.

At its core, this chapter will highlight how white supremacy functions as a tool of power in educational spaces, shaping discipline policies, parental engagement, and overall student success. Despite decades of equity efforts, many classrooms remain spaces where power and privilege disproportionately harm students of color.

I will also explore how well-meaning white liberals often believe they are simply "upholding the rules," when in reality, their actions reinforce white supremacy and create additional barriers for Black and Brown families to fully engage in their children's education. This chapter concludes with discussion questions and action steps to help educators interrogate their own biases, advocate for systemic change, and create truly inclusive school environments that center the humanity of all students and families.

Most recently, the term "Karen" has been widely used in popular culture and memes to describe white individuals who call the police on Black people for everyday activities or take it upon themselves to enforce rules that do not exist, often under the guise of maintaining order or preventing wrongdoing. These actions reflect a broader pattern of racialized surveillance and control, where Black individuals are unjustly scrutinized and policed in their daily lives.

Professor Apryl Williams (2020) of the University of Michigan has demonstrated that these memes are a type of cultural analysis, critique, and rejection of white women's "surveillance and regulation of Black bodies in public spaces-making an important connection between racialized surveillance of the past and contemporary acts of 'casual racism'" (p. 11).

Applying Dr. Williams' analysis, I argue that these acts of casual racism occur daily in schools across the country, where school officials attempt to regulate Black and Brown students' behavior and presence. This over-regulation is an extension of how the white gaze normalizes racism within educational spaces. While this "casual racism" is often framed as "school rules," the reality is that failing to see students through a humanized lens deepens educational inequities—leaving a group of students underprepared, unwelcome, and disconnected from their learning environments.

Furthermore, the concept of "Karen" has been further explored in popular culture, most notably in Beyoncé's highly anticipated seventh studio album, Renaissance, released in July 2022. In the track "Energy," Beyoncé continues her tradition of using music as a form of social commentary, addressing public issues—including the pervasive nature of racial entitlement and surveillance. In the song, Beyoncé says:

> We was chillin', mindin' our business Poppin' our pain and champagne through the ceiling Sippin' it up, flickin' it up All this good energy got you all in your feelings, feelings I'm crazy, I'm swearin' I'm darin', your man starin' I just entered the country with Derringers 'Cause them Karens just turned into terrorists.

Here, Beyoncé demonstrates the extent to which Black Joy is scrutinized by white surveillance, so much so that when Black people are simply minding their business, celebrating, and exuding great energy, that energy is met with hostility. Karens weaponize this scrutiny, policing Black existence and disrupting moments of joy. This same sentiment is often replicated in schools, where Black students are often seen as too loud and disrespectful—labels that often result in disproportionate discipline. To fully understand the Karen phenomenon, we have to start with social media examples of white supremacy in action—instances where Black people are just enjoying their daily lives and are often surveilled, policed, and punished by white individuals who deem themselves as authorities to pursue justice on behalf of the public.

Oakland Cookout Karen

On April 29, 2018, a Black family in Oakland, CA, was cooking out/barbecuing at Lake Merritt, a well-known community gathering place. According to the city's website, Lake Merritt is the "Jewel of Oakland." It is a massive lake that covers 155 acres of land surrounded by green space, wildlife, a Nature Center, Gardens, Parks, Jogging path, Tennis Courts, Boating Center, Libraries, and a children's Fairyland. The lake is a diverse, urban public space that regularly hosts community events, including a weekly farmers market.

On that day, an unidentified white woman called the police on two Black men barbecuing, because the type of grill they used required charcoal. According to one of the men, Mr. Kenzie Smith, he was setting up his grill as he had done for many years. According to a news report from KRON4, "She said that we were trespassing, we were not welcome, and then she turned back around and said, 'ya'll going to jail,'" said Smith. When the woman called the police, no one was arrested. The incident was recorded, and the moment went viral. The woman who called the police was dubbed "BBQ Becky."

In response, the Oakland community organized a resistance event—BBQing While Black—just one month later. Nearly 2,000 people attended, transforming the act of barbecuing into a powerful statement of Black Joy, resistance, and reclamation. Living in spaces where Black people are constantly surveilled, questioned about their right to belong, and subjected to police intervention makes the ability to experience joy even more revolutionary. Jhamel Robinson, a co-organizer of the event, described its significance: "This is a beautiful cultural event. It's to bring the whole city out with love and peace" (Fox 2 KTVU, 2018).

Central Park Karen

According to NPR's WAMU 88.5, "It has gone on to become one of the most widely publicized so-called 'Karen' incidents, where a white person, typically a woman, calls police to report a Black or brown person engaged in mundane activities" (NPR WAMU, February 2021). During this May 2021 incident, Amy Cooper allowed her unleashed dog to walk around the park when she encountered Christian Cooper who asked her to put her dog on a leash. Ms. Cooper received backlash as she called the police on Mr. Cooper for no reason. In the viral video, she can be heard saying, "There's an African-American man threatening my life," simply because he asked her to comply with park rules. The footage quickly spread online, leading to Amy Cooper's termination from her job at investment firm Franklin Templeton, which cited her actions as the reason for dismissal. The incident led Amy Cooper to file a lawsuit, claiming she was wrongfully terminated due to "condemnations of racism." She was fired the day after the incident, with her employer stating, "We do not tolerate racism of any kind." In June 2023, Reuters reported that Cooper lost her lawsuit against the company. Franklin Templeton maintained its stance, stating, "We continue to believe the company responded appropriately" (Reuters, 2023).

These incidents happen continuously. The ones I'm highlighting for you are the ones that have created a larger conversation for how white supremacy functions and when people use whiteness for what they believe will benefit them. In these examples, women that identify and present as white, meaning their skin is white and their hair aligns with societal norms of whiteness ("straight" or without curl), is typically what is akin to whiteness. These women often use their perceived authority to call the police.

From what we know, these calls frequently escalate, leading to Black and Brown people being unlawfully arrested or, in the worst cases, subject to violence or death. In schools, when people call the school police or a higher authority on kids, we recognize that they are more likely to be punished and or injured as a result. Subscribing to whiteness/white supremacy in these incidents means that being white is synonymous with authority.

When someone who is white calls another authority figure, the assumption is that their version of events will be believed. While white supremacy is often equated with white people, it is, more accurately, a societal tool associated with power. The closer someone is perceived to be to whiteness, the more protection and privilege they receive. Conversely, those who are farther from whiteness are more vulnerable to surveillance, control, and harm. We see this pattern continue in the next example with Soho Karen.

Soho Karen

When the idea for this book first emerged in 2020, I was at home with my two young children, immersed in the racial reckoning unfolding before us. The world was watching what Black people had long known and experienced—white supremacy's deep-rooted impact on society. But this time, it was unavoidable, broadcast on television and social media for all to see. With everyone stuck at home due to Covid-19, people suddenly had the time to reflect, to learn how to support Black businesses, and to reckon with their own complicity in systemic racism.

And yet, while some things have changed, much remains the same. The phenomenon of "Karen" continues to manifest in different spaces, even if the viral terminology isn't as widely used as it was in 2020. White supremacy does not simply fade away; it must be actively resisted and dismantled. This is something I emphasize to my students all the time: while they may take one diversity course in college, the real work requires a lifelong commitment to disruption.

Now, as public schools face attacks and the very idea of diversity is being framed as a societal "problem," we need more than just people declaring, "I am not racist." We have heard that before. What we need are individuals who are deeply committed to seeing the children and families they serve as fully human—just as worthy of care, compassion, and advocacy as their own loved ones. I'm talking about the kind of love that moves us to action when a family member is struggling, the empathy that compels us to listen and support a friend in need, and the instinct to give the benefit of the doubt rather than rely on harmful stereotypes.

We must retrain our minds and hearts to center humanity. Before we can effectively disrupt white supremacy, we need to recognize how it operates—how "Karen" behavior and systemic racism show up in schools, youth organizations, and everyday interactions. Only then can we begin the necessary work of dismantling these structures and creating truly equitable spaces for all.

Karen's Impact in Schools

White supremacy in schools is not often what we think. When we think of white supremacy, we may think of overt signs in schools and community centers that read "whites only." Instead, it manifests in everyday interactions—quiet conversations among teachers, the reinforcement of harmful stereotypes, and the ways colleagues treat students and educators of colors. It is embedded in low expectations, differential discipline, and the systemic barriers that determine who is seen as capable and who is not.

When I was in my first year of teaching, I was always encouraged to "just write them up" or I was told not to give "those" students any real assignments because "they won't do them." As an eager new teacher, I was disheartened to be told by white administrators and my department chair that this was simply the culture of the school. Nearly twenty years later, those words still stick with me.

I taught five classes, including one section of honors World History at a large public high school. My experience there was eye-opening and motivated me to better understand the realities of Black students and their families in educational spaces. The expectations for Black students were noticeably lower. A department teacher told me outright that "they" wouldn't put in the effort. Meanwhile, Black students were written up for even minor infractions—such as being late to class—at much higher rates than their white peers.

Many of my Black students, juniors and seniors, shared their aspirations of going to college. They wanted the same opportunities as their white counterparts in my honors class. However, there was a stark difference—white students had been guided into honors courses as early as ninth grade, backed by school employees who believed in their academic potential. The Black students, placed in so-called "regular" classes, had never been advised to take the necessary prerequisites for college. It wasn't until our conversations that they even realized what they had been missing.

This is the reality in many schools—the assumption that "those" kids are not capable of excelling. The harmful belief that Black families don't care about their children's education persists, despite overwhelming evidence to the contrary. Time and time again, we see cases in the media where school officials engage in racist behaviors that impact children's educational experiences and life trajectories. If we are to truly dismantle white supremacy in schools, we must first acknowledge that it exists—not just in blatant acts of discrimination but in the quiet, insidious ways expectations, access, and discipline are unequally distributed. There have been several cases where school officials have demonstrated racist behaviors toward children in educational spaces.

When reading the following case studies, remember the American Psychological Association's definition of racism and racial discrimination:

- Racism: *n.* A system of structuring opportunity and assigning value based on phenotypic properties (e.g., skin color and hair texture associated with "race" in the United States), which ranges from daily interpersonal interactions shaped by race to racialized opportunities for good education, housing, employment, and other resources, and unfairly disadvantages people belonging to marginalized racial groups. Racism is a form of prejudice that generally includes negative emotional reactions to members of the group, acceptance of negative stereotypes, and racial discrimination against individuals; in some cases it leads to violence.

- Racial discrimination: The differential treatment of individuals because of their membership in a particular racial group. Discrimination is in most cases the behavioral manifestation of prejudice and therefore involves unfair, negative, hostile, or injurious treatment.

Case Studies in Schools

Case Study 1: White Principal in Chicago Calling DSS for Minor Lateness

In May 2021, JaNay Dodson, Black mom and teacher at Hyde Park Academy in Chicago Public School, realized the school bus with her son who attended Inter-American Magnet School also in Chicago Public Schools was going to be late. Ms. Dodson was teaching online that day as she waited for her son to come home on the bus. According to a report from WGN 9 News in Chicago (WGN-TV, 2021), "I was expecting him to be on the school bus," Dodson said. "He signed up for transportation. There were some issues with some of the routes being canceled."

After she realized that he wasn't going to make it home on the bus, she attempted to call the school. After trying several times, there was no answer. Ms. Dodson called her brother to pick up her son, and he arrived at 4:37 p.m., which was seven minutes late according to the school policy of picking up students at 4:30 p.m. The next day the principal, a white woman, Dr. Daniela Bylaitis, emailed Ms. Dodson and let her know students needed to be picked up by 4:30 p.m. or the Department of Children and Family Services (DCFS) would be called as they don't have the staff to monitor the children. However, the principal didn't indicate that she, in fact, had already called DCFS.

A representative of the department interviewed the student at school and inquired where he lived. Ms. Dodson reported to WGN9, "He just ran and gave me a hug and was like 'I'm so dumb,' I said, 'baby, why are you dumb?' He said, 'I shouldn't have told her when she said where I live. I should have said nope, that's not it because she can just come to our home now and come get me'" (WGN-TV, 2021). The actions of the principal led to community outrage. People organized to have the policy reexamined. A month after the event occurred, Reporter Jake Wittich of Block Club Chicago. com reported that the principal had resigned effective immediately due to pressure from the local community and parents. According to the article, she voluntarily transitioned into a "non-school-based role" at Chicago Public Schools according to a CPS spokesperson

(Wittich, 2021). Looking at this case, you may ask yourself, how is this racist or racially discriminating?

When we review the history of how schools and organizations respond to Black mothers, they are not typically given the benefit of the doubt; instead, policies are often enforced against them with rigidity rather than compassion. This stems from deeply ingrained narratives portraying Black mothers as unfit, as people who exploit the system, rely on public assistance, are lazy, and have too many children or have an "attitude." These harmful stereotypes have been reinforced through government policies and media for generations.

So, when a school principal decides that calling the DCFS is more appropriate than simply calling a mother, it is rooted in racism. Instead of escalating the situation to child protective services, a simple phone call could have provided clarity. A conversation with the mother or even the student's uncle—who did pick him up— could have resolved the issue without unnecessary trauma.

The humane approach in any situation like this is to first understand what is happening. A simple conversation could have revealed the circumstances and prevented the need for punitive measures. Educators must approach situations with a *spirit of care* and *understanding* versus a mindset of punishment. The decision to involve DCFS left a lasting impact on the family, causing unnecessary distress and trauma.

I ask you to put yourself in this situation—imagine the fear of being taken from your home and loving parents over a minor misunderstanding. In my twenty years as an educator, I have seen children from all backgrounds, including those from the most challenging circumstances and those from wealthier families. And what I have learned is this: things happen.

I remember waiting with a student after basketball practice one evening. All of the other students had left, but she and I waited for her mother. Her mother, a local restaurant owner, was in a rush to come pick her up. She shared that something that came up and she was deeply apologetic. I knew this family. I never thought to call child protective services. I have also encountered families experiencing temporary housing, struggling with transportation issues that occasionally made them late to pick up their children. In that instance, I made a phone call, and we made a plan to get them home. I did not default to calling child protective services.

Building relationships with students' families is key. Being flexible and centering humanity should always come first. Instead of rigidly enforcing punitive policies, schools should ask:

- How can we support families facing challenges?
- Could the school assist in arranging bus transportation for the student?
- Could staff ensure that someone is available to answer last-minute emergency calls at dismissal?
- Could phone calls be redirected to a cell phone if a staff member is unavailable at a landline?
- Could text messaging be used to contact parents directly?

These small, proactive steps would prevent unnecessary escalations and build trust between schools and the families they serve. Ultimately, we must recognize that many policies are deeply rooted in racist structures, and the default should never be punishment. Instead, we must center humanity and understanding in every interaction.

Case Study 2: White School Employee Forced Black Child to Eat Food Out of Trash Can

In a December 2021 article of a local Ohio news station, the headline read: *Superintendent fires principal, staffer after child allegedly forced to eat food from garbage.* The report outlines how a Black girl in the fourth grade was given two options for breakfast in the school cafeteria. She was not happy with the food choices. She approached the trash can to throw it away and attempted to retrieve another choice. A white woman school employee, on surveillance camera, told the young student to get a paper towel and to retrieve the food from the trash can. According to the lawsuit, the family indicated the child became sick and was humiliated in front of the peers that were laughing at her. As stated in the report:

> According to the suit, the student developed a fever and was taken to a doctor. Additionally, the student has had to undergo mental health treatment for the "humiliating actions" and her Fourteenth Amendment

rights were violated. "This isn't another student trying to convince them to do something silly or to eat something, this is an educator punishing this girl by forcing her to eat garbage," said attorney Jared Klevanow who filed the lawsuit. (News 5 Cleveland, 2021)

After the investigation, upon suggestion of the school board, the principal and paraprofessional were both fired from the school. This is another instance where white people believe it's more important to force the "rules" or punish a child for not being "grateful" for the food they are given.

They forced a child to be humiliated, and to create trauma for the child, rather than recognizing the humanity of the child. Even as adults, we dislike certain foods that are given to us. In fact, etiquette classes teach socially acceptable ways to discard food you dislike—how to use your fork to discreetly remove food, how to indicate to staff that we are finished, or how to decline a dish altogether. This level of grace, however, is not extended to Black children or children of color.

Monique Morris describes in her book (2016) how Black girls often experience criminalization in school, in disproportionate ways and calls for schools to be sites of healing for Black girls. In this case, there is no justification for the adults' behavior.

Forcing a child to retrieve food from the trash is dehumanizing and punitive. It is not our place to dictate what children should or should not eat. Nor is it acceptable to force a child to retrieve discarded food as a consequence for their choice. Centering humanity means placing ourselves in the students' position. If we, as adults, choose not to eat certain foods, no one forces us to. So why is a child denied that same dignity? What harm would there have been in allowing the student to try a different meal? Instead of making assumptions, the adults in this situation could have simply asked questions to understand what the child needed. A basic act of compassion could have prevented unnecessary trauma.

Case Study 3: California Teacher Unknowingly Recording Racist Comments about Black Parents on Zoom

In April of 2021, according to NBC News.com story, Katura Stokes, a mom of a sixth-grade student in Palmdale, California, was having difficulty accessing the school's online platform for remote learning. This is something that we saw a lot of during the pandemic. Ms. Stokes scheduled a meeting with her son's science teacher, Ms. Kimberly Newman. The meeting between the teacher and the parent was held on Zoom. After the meeting, the teacher did not turn off her microphone and said:

> "Your son has learned to lie to everybody and make excuses," Newman apparently says on the recording. "Because you've taught him to make excuses that nothing is his fault. This is what Black people do. This is what Black people do. White people do it, too, but Black people do it way more." She continues with "These parents, that's what kinds of pieces of s--- they are," Newman says. "Black. He's Black. They're a Black family." (NBC News, 2021)

Ms. Stokes recorded the racist rant and called the school's principal. Even after the principal called, the teacher denied saying any of the insults, despite the mother's recording.

The teacher was put on administrative leave, and within a few days, the teacher resigned. The family pursued a lawsuit for personal injuries accusing the Palmdale School District of inflicting emotional distress, defamation. and violations of the Civil Rights Act. In this case, the teacher was recorded, and the family was able to pursue justice. Once again, we see a white teacher openly expressing discrimination and prejudice toward a Black family—this time, simply because they sought assistance with the online learning platform during the pandemic.

In my research of the experience of frontline workers, Black mothers indicated that many teachers never communicated that their child was at academic risk—they only found out when grades were posted. The pandemic highlighted communication challenges, particularly for Black families.

We know the pandemic created hardships for many. However, if we approach this case study from a humanity-centered perspective, we would simply see a mom and student who needed the teacher's assistance. A teacher who embraced grace and compassion would recognize that everyone navigated unprecedented challenges. Perhaps the student was using unfamiliar technology. Many students who lacked their own personal devices relied on school-issued technology. Research shows that Black and other marginalized families are more likely to access homework and important school resources via mobile devices.

Rather than viewing the mother's outreach as a burden, the teacher could have recognized it as a positive sign—an engaged parent advocating for their child's education. Instead, the response inflicted unnecessary trauma on both the mother and the child. Educators must do better. Offering the benefit of the doubt rather than defaulting to harmful assumptions about Black families—assumptions rooted in racism—should be the standard, not the exception.

White Supremacy as a Tool in Education

The case studies above highlight how white women—who make up the majority of school staff—often engage in racist and discriminatory behaviors that are not isolated incidents but rather part of a larger systemic issue in schools. These instances reveal a profound lack of humanity. In each case, these women have positioned themselves as arbiters of morality, deciding what the moral compass of Black students should look like.

While the concept of "Karen" behavior has been popularized through memes, these viral moments document something far more insidious—white supremacy in action. The harm inflicted is not just about individual actions but about a broader system that consistently devalues Black students and families, treating them as less deserving of dignity, care, and basic human respect.

Exploring White Educators' Use of Power and Privilege

The field of education is predominantly led by white women, particularly in public schools, where they make up the majority of classroom teachers and administrators. For decades, efforts have been made to encourage these educators to become more culturally responsive, inclusive, and competent. However, data continues to show that Black students are disproportionately suspended and pushed out of school at higher rates than their white counterparts, even in districts where white students make up the majority population. Additionally, when examining nonprofit organizations tasked with filling the gaps for Black youth and other students of color—providing services such as tutoring, college access, and youth development—these organizations are overwhelmingly led by white individuals. According to Candid.org, in a 2024 article entitled *"Did nonprofit leadership become more racially diverse after 2020?"* the article revealed,

> There were no major shifts in the overall racial representation of nonprofit CEOs at the sector level. Looking at each year of data in aggregate, the racial distributions of nonprofit CEOs remained consistent from year to year. Nonprofit CEOs are predominantly white: More than 70 percent of organizations are led by a white CEO. On average, only 13 percent of nonprofit CEOs identify as Black/African American, while just 6 percent are Hispanic/Latinx and 4 percent are Asian American/Pacific Islander. Native American is the least represented race/ethnicity, accounting for less than 1 percent of CEOs each year. (Candid 2024, May 2)

Given that leadership in both schools and nonprofits serving children is predominantly white, it is imperative for educators in these spaces to engage in reflective practices that push back against white supremacy and explore policies and how they affect families. Over the years, I have consulted with many groups and witnessed firsthand how these policies disproportionately impact Black families daily. From zero tolerance disciplinary policies to removing Black families from programs due to transportation barriers, the consequences are far-reaching.

In one of the mentoring programs I evaluated, I observed white mentors excluding Black mothers from discussions about mentoring plans. These mothers expressed feeling excluded and wanted direct communication with the mentors, whom they felt disrespected them. The mentors, on the other hand, believed they were providing an opportunity to re-parent these children, assuming the parents had not done their best raising them. This belief—that educators or program leaders are more knowledgeable or morally superior to Black parents—is deeply rooted in white supremacy. Historically, Black parents have been deemed as not capable, not worthy of how they raise their own children, and their work obligations have been misinterpreted as a lack of care rather than a reflection of systemic inequities.

Both school and out-of-school program leaders must be intentional about the values they uphold and the messages they send through their policies and interactions. It is essential to center the experiences of Black families, actively work against ingrained biases, and take deliberate steps to dismantle the harmful narratives that perpetuate white supremacy.

Well-Meaning White People and Racism

In this chapter, I outlined the cases of *Karen* in both social media and actual events in public spaces and schools. However, while many may label these instances as overt racism, sociologist Barbara Trepagnier found in her study that well-meaning white women either demonstrated or acknowledged what she describes as "silent racism." According to Trepagnier:

> Silent racism refers to the shared images and assumptions of members of the dominant group about subordinate groups—that is, the shared images and assumptions held by white Americans about Black Americans and other people of color. This line of thinking leads to scrutiny of an erroneous way of thinking about racism prevalent in the minds of many, including racial progressives: the idea that people are either racist or not racist. The study of silent racism sought out well-meaning white women willing to talk about their own racism. The approach required openness about a topic that is rarely discussed, and yet people were eager to join the study. Twenty-five women participated in eight focus groups and kept their thoughts about racism in a journal for three weeks following their discussion. Their stories indicate that silent racism does exist in the minds of well-meaning white people. Participants either acknowledged their own silent racism or demonstrated it in the study, indicating that the not racist category is both inaccurate and deceptive. (Trepagnier, 2001, p. 354)

I suggest that our approach to addressing racism in schools and youth-focused spaces has often centered on trying to help individuals step away from their racist beliefs and behaviors. However, as Trepagnier has suggested, racism is not a simple binary of being racist or not. Instead, well-meaning white people often subscribe to silent racism—a set of shared images and assumptions about Black Americans that shape their actions, often unconsciously. These assumptions frequently lead to the very behaviors I have described. As a reader, it is up to you to actively work toward dismantling the silent racism in your own thinking. This requires deliberate engagement with the students and families you serve, fostering genuine relationships, and committing to a practice of continuous reflection and growth.

Steps for Action and Reflection

The importance of action and reflection as an educator can't be underestimated. While many educators take a class on the diversity of schools or attend workshops on working with students of color, those are not enough. As you have read, the notion of "Karen" manifests in the everydayness of life. Black families and youth are constantly under surveillance, whether at a park, Zoom meetings, college dorms, grocery stores, and walking in neighborhoods. This level of scrutiny is so common in educational settings, it is often mistaken for school discipline. These harsh realities impact the daily lives of Black folks in public spaces and youth in educational settings.

In order for us to move past this, educators and youth workers must be intentional about disrupting white supremacy. I have witnessed this firsthand in my graduate course, where white graduate students, many for the first time, are confronted with what it means to be to white in the American South while working in predominantly Black educational spaces. The resistance I encountered from these students often stems from their discomfort with being in a majority-Black environment. In these cases, these students are often preparing to remain in our local school district, which is predominantly Black and Latinx.

I spend a significant time reminding my students that their role as educators is to center on the humanity of the students they are serving. I emphasize that their work is not about control, superiority, or maintaining the status quo, but about teaching with empathy, care, and compassion. Without this fundamental shift in perspective, we cannot dismantle the racialized hierarchies that continue to harm Black students and families.

In order for white people to move past their own insecurities around teaching students unlike them, they must do the following:

1. Reflect on your own upbringing and understanding of the world.

While your experiences of the world are unique, you will need to interrogate where your values align with your current experiences and where you have room for growth for a new perspective.

2. Build genuine relationships with students.

When you begin working with your students, get to know them. Do one-on-one interviews where you find out about their interests and family values. Continue those conversations throughout your time with them. Consider it an ongoing process. Start this at the beginning of the school year and continue to check in with students and their families monthly to stay connected and responsive to their evolving needs.

3. Create access to resources and opportunities.

What opportunities can you create networking for your students and their families to learn about information that often is not shared with them openly? Are there opportunities for scholarships, tutoring, community opportunities, housing support, and food resources? These resources are often withheld from families and often navigating how to survive can be helpful.

4. Advocate with empathy and service.

Build relationships with a mind of advocacy and service with the intersection of empathy. Building relationships allows the students and families to be in a reciprocal relationship and that can only begin with building a relationship of trust.

5. Challenge harmful narratives and stereotypes.

Where can you find opportunities to support and advocate for Black students in your organization? Advocacy also means speaking up when you hear colleagues repeating harmful stereotypes about students and families. Use the truths you've learned from building relationships to counter misinformation and bias. When opportunities arise that could benefit students, actively work to connect them with the resources and support they need.

6. Prioritize communication and de-escalation over punitive measures.

When you are in positions of leadership or authority, how can the use of intentional and open communication be used to come to an understanding when challenges arise? Instead of the impulse of calling a higher authority, can there be de-escalation techniques involved? Can you learn more about what the tension may be? Most of the time parents and students who have reached a point of frustration have not had the opportunity to share those frustrations. Creating space for dialogue can prevent unnecessary disciplinary actions and build stronger community ties.

Implications for Fostering an Inclusive and Equitable Learning Environment

To foster an inclusive and equitable environment, it's important to start by examining your own beliefs about Black people and communities of color. When you think of families, what initial stereotypes come to mind? A critical first step is disrupting those harmful stereotypes which are often shaped by media representation and societal messaging. Instead of relying on those harmful stereotypes, shift your perspective to see students and families as individuals striving for a good life—people who, like anyone else, want the very best for their children and communities. To better understand what that looks like for them, building authentic relationships with your students and their families is essential.

Ways to Foster Stronger Connections

- Hosting events in your space that allow for informal conversations, offering some snacks and creating a caring, inviting space that encourages open conversations.
- Engage in one-on-one meetings with families to discuss their hopes, dreams, and how you can support them in achieving those dreams and goals.
- Leverage your network to connect students and families with opportunities, mentorship, or resources aligned with their interests.
- Create an open line of communication by using a communication tool or app that allows you to share updates and positive moments, such as pictures of student achievements.
- Learn about students' interests and incorporate books, discussions, or activities that align with those interests to foster deeper engagement.

Understanding the history of unjust practices that students in the community may have been subjected to, in terms of unjust discipline policies, treatment of parents in school communication and policies, and how the population has been treated by local school systems, can help you navigate relationships with greater awareness and empathy.

As we saw with the Chicago school principal's rigid enforcement of "policy," prioritizing rules over relationships can result in trauma and deep mistrust. By giving families the opportunity to share their concerns, you create the foundation for better relationships. Recognizing families as knowledge holders and valuable partners in the learning process will ultimately lead to more inclusive and supportive programming.

Discussion Questions

1. In what ways can you critically reflect on your own privilege, particularly as it relates to whiteness?
2. How has this privilege shaped your experiences in educational settings?
3. The chapter discusses the concept of well-meaning white liberal "niceness." How can you actively disrupt the reliance on whiteness and niceness as a default mode of engagement in educational spaces? What actions can you take to move beyond performative allyship?
4. Reflecting on the families you work with, how has white supremacy impacted their experiences in educational settings? Where do you see opportunities to advocate for them in meaningful ways? How can you use your position to challenge inequitable policies or practices?

References

Online News Articles:

Blumer, H. (1958). "Race prejudice as a sense of group position." *Pacific Sociological Review, 1*(1), 3–7.

Candid. (2024, May 2). *Did Nonprofit Leadership Become More Racially Diverse After 2020?* Candid. https://blog.candid.org/post/is-nonprofit-leadership-more-diverse-after-2020-demographic-data-insights/.

KTVU. (2018, May). *'Bringing the Whole City Out:' BBQing While Black at Lake Merritt Draws Diverse Crowds.* KTVU. https://www.ktvu.com/news/bringing-the-whole-city-out-bbqing-while-black-at-lake-merritt-draws-diverse-crowds.

National Public Radio (NPR). (2021, February 16). *Amy Cooper, White Woman Who Called Police on Black Bird-watcher, Has Charge Dismissed.* NPR. https://www.npr.org/2021/02/16/968372253/white-woman-who-called-police-on-black-man-bird-watching-has-charges-dismissed.

NBC News. (2021, April). *Teacher Goes on Racist Rant, Not Realizing Zoom Was On, Mother of Black Child Says.* NBC News. https://www.nbcnews.com/news/us-news/teacher-goes-racist-rant-after-not-realizing-zoom-was-mother-n1262843.

News 5 Cleveland. (2021). *Parent Sues Lorain City Schools after Child Allegedly Forced to Eat Out of Garbage Can.* https://www.news5cleveland.com/news/local-news/parent-sues-lorain-city-schools-after-child-allegedly-forced-to-eat-out-of-garbage-can.

New York Times. (2020, July 31). *A Brief History of 'Karen'.* https://www.nytimes.com/2020/07/31/style/karen-name-meme-history.html.

Reuters. (2023, June 8). *Woman Who Called Police on Black Bird-watcher in Central Park Loses Employment Appeal.* Reuters. https://www.reuters.com/world/us/woman-who-called-police-black-bird-watcher-central-park-loses-employment-appeal-2023-06-08/.

WGN-TV. (2021). *CPS Policy Questioned after DCFS Called on Mom Late Picking Up Son.* https://wgntv.com/news/chicago-news/cps-policy-questioned-after-dcfs-called-on-mom-late-picking-up-son/.

Wittich, J. (2021, April 28). *Lakeview Principal Who Reported Black Mom to DCFS Quits after Weeks of Pressure from Parents.* Retrieved from https://blockclubchicago.org/2021/04/28/lakeview-principal-who-reported-black-mom-to-dcfs-quits-after-weeks-of-pressure-from-parents/

Books and Academic Sources:

hooks, b. (1995). *Killing Rage: Ending Racism.* H. Holt and Co.

Morris, M. (2016). *Pushout: The Criminalization of Black Girls in Schools.* The New Press.

Trepagnier, B. (2011). "Silent Racism." In *Covert Racism,* 353–64. Brill.

Williams, A. (2020). "Black Memes Matter:# LivingWhileBlack with Becky and Karen." *Social Media+ Society,* 6 (4): 2056305120981047.

Dictionaries and Online Definitions:

American Psychological Association. (n.d.). *Racial Discrimination.* In *APA Dictionary of Psychology.* https://dictionary.apa.org/racial-discrimination.

American Psychological Association. (n.d.). *Racism.* In *APA Dictionary of Psychology.* https://dictionary.apa.org/racism.

Not everything that is faced can be changed, but nothing can be changed until it is faced.

—James Baldwin

Introduction

The purpose of this chapter is to provide educators with a framework that will inspire and support them in developing anti-racist practices with students and their families. This chapter introduces a conceptual framework I developed called *Reflection for Humanity*, designed to guide educators in continuous self-examination and growth. This framework is not meant to be a one-time professional development session or a single reading experience. Instead, it encourages ongoing reflection and engagement throughout an educator's career.

As you read this chapter I am asking you to do the "work" ongoing and continuously. This is a mind shift. At its core, Reflection for Humanity challenges educators to rethink their role from one of neutral being to that of an active participant in shaping just and equitable learning environments. It requires you to deeply reflect and push yourself beyond your comfort zone, challenge the status quo, and recognize that being an anti-racist educator is not simply about you not being racist, rather it is about committing to the work of liberation for people beyond racism.

This framework is especially crucial in the current political and social climate, where efforts to dismantle diversity, equity, and inclusion, also known more as DEI, policies threaten to undo decades of progress.

These rollbacks disproportionately harm historically marginalized communities, reinforcing the need for educators to center humanity in their work. In response, Reflection for Humanity provides a structured approach for educators to actively engage in dismantling racism and fostering an environment where all students and families can thrive.

One of the biggest challenges in education is the misconception that diversity training or equity workshops are sufficient to create meaningful change. Too often, educators attend a single professional development session and leave with unanswered questions, such as "But how do I actually implement this?" Similarly, I have had white graduate students tell me they feel unqualified to work with Black students because they did not grow up in racially diverse environments. This highlights the flawed notion that equity work can be achieved through isolated workshops rather than through a mindset shift and sustained commitment.

Being an anti-racist, humanity-centered educator requires more than passive learning—it demands intentional action and continuous reflection. It means actively recognizing and addressing racial injustices, both in the classroom and in broader educational policies. It means consistently seeing and valuing students and their families as full human beings, worthy of dignity, respect, and equitable opportunities.

As you engage with this framework, I encourage you to approach it not as a checklist, but as an ongoing practice—one that evolves as society presents new challenges and injustices. The work of anti-racism is never finished, but through deep reflection, sustained effort, and a commitment to justice, educators can become catalysts for real, transformative change.

The Reflection for Humanity Framework: An Overview

The first point on the framework is *Do the Work*. This point calls on educators to engage in deep self-reflection. Ask yourself the following questions:

1. Who am I?
2. How are my personal beliefs informed?
3. How are my power and privilege reflected in my daily interactions?
4. As an anti-racist educator, where can I challenge my own biases and assumptions?

The second point on the framework is *Whose Story Is Being Told?* This prong challenges educators to critically examine the narratives they uphold in their work—from lesson plans, to meetings, to the local news they take in daily. Ask yourself:

1. Who is getting priority and who is being neglected?
2. Are the perspectives of marginalized communities being silenced or distorted?
3. Are these narratives based on racist assumptions or exclusionary frameworks?

The third prong is *How Is the Story Being Told and Who Benefits?* asks educators to assess the impact of these narratives. Are they reinforcing white supremacy, or are they challenging dominant power structures? When stories elevate only white voices and omit the experiences of marginalized groups, they reinforce systemic inequities. These narratives shape society's understanding of race, contributing to disparities in education, healthcare, and housing—issues that deeply affect students inside and outside of school.

The final prong on the framework is *Take Action—Steps for Humanity*. This part of the framework is where educators move beyond reflection and commit to action. Anti-racist teaching requires intentional, sustained efforts to dismantle systemic inequities. Educators must:

- Challenge racist policies and practices within their schools
- Advocate for marginalized students and their families
- Engage with their communities to amplify underrepresented voices
- Move beyond their own comfort zones to create meaningful change

By implementing this framework, educators can go beyond passive allyship and take concrete steps toward equity and justice in their classrooms and beyond.

First Prong: Do the Work (Self-Reflection and Identity Analysis)

This work will require critical reflection. When working in people-centered roles, we must be intentional about reflection, recognizing what feels *normal* to us may not be *normal* to others. In order to better understand who you are, you must take time to sit with your thoughts, reflect, and remain open to growth. As educators, we often carry preconceived ideas of who we want to be or who we hope not to become.

When I first started teaching, I walked into my social studies classroom, wanting to be a perfect mix of my tenth-grade English teacher and my history professor from the University of Chicago. I was inspired by both of them. My tenth-grade English teacher, Ms. Duffener, pushed me to think and required all of us to be critical thinkers. She taught us how to highlight the book, how to write in the margins, and how to take notes. She encouraged us to look at symbolism. I had never experienced a course like hers and it left a deep impact on me.

I was also inspired by my graduate school history professor, Thomas Holt. Professor Holt pushed me to become a better writer but with a kindness that I also had never experienced. His teaching was impressive; the material we covered in his African American History to 1877 class was thought-provoking and presented information in a way that was most interesting to me and inspiring as a Black woman. It was in that course that I first learned of Olaudah Equiano, an African man who details his experiences in a book: *The Interesting Narrative of the Life of Olaudah Equiano.* In this text, he recounts his journey from enslavement to securing his freedom in Britain. Reading his story was a transformative experience for me, as I had never encountered it before. When I began teaching social studies in Florida, I made sure to share this text with my students.

For many of us that pursue higher education, we are inevitably inspired by our own coaches, teachers, afterschool program leaders, Boys and Girls club instructors, and other impactful adults. Beyond inspirational, these are often the people who highly influenced our decision to become educators. To begin the task of moving beyond inspiration to action, we have to embark on a journey of self-understanding.

Understanding Yourself as an Educator

To understand yourself as an educator, you must recognize how your identity shapes the way you engage in classrooms, afterschool programs, community organizations, Boys and Girls Clubs, and sports teams. I encourage you to take time for reflection before your program begins—whether in the summer or during pre-planning. Set aside a moment to write or type responses to the following questions, using them as a guide for self-awareness and growth.

1. *Who am I?*

When answering these questions, consider your broader identity including gender, race, and the region of the country you are from. Are you a sibling? What is your economic status? What is your ability status? Understanding *who* you are and how you describe yourself will help inform your response to the next question.

2. *How are my personal beliefs formed?*

Did you grow up in a religious home? Were you the oldest child in your family? Did you come from divorced parents? Did you grow up in a homogeneous neighborhood? These factors all influence *how* we think about the world. Did you grow up with the belief that children should be seen and not heard? Were you taught that the teacher is always right? These beliefs, shaped by our upbringing and life experiences, influence not only how we see ourselves, but also how we *should* engage with the world. Our personal experiences shape how we treat others and the assumptions we hold about different groups of people.

3. *How do my power and privilege manifest daily?*

When we think of privilege, discussions often focus on factors like wealth, race, and gender. However, it is important to reframe privilege in the context of situations and people we encounter daily. For example, you may believe that you do not necessarily have privilege based on how much money you have; however, is your privilege situated in your educational attainment? Is it in your access to healthcare? Is it in the job you hold? Recognizing privilege beyond its most commonly discussed forms allows us to better understand our position in relation to the people we serve, fostering greater awareness and empathy.

4. *Where do I have gaps in my understanding?*

When we look at who we are and who we serve as educators, there is always room for growth and understanding. If you are serving a group of predominantly marginalized students—what knowledge gaps might you have? If you approach the world from a white perspective, what gaps might exist when working with someone who sees the world through a Black or Hispanic lens? If you are able-bodied, how might your understanding be limited when working with students who have disabilities? This is an important step in self-reflection. It may feel uncomfortable, but I encourage you to sit with that discomfort and lean into it. Instead of resisting, consider: What perspectives can your students offer you? What can you learn from them?

Recognizing implicit biases and working toward self-awareness is only achievable once we really sit and reflect on where we stand. It is important to complete this step because it opens the door for growth and a clearer understanding of where to do the work. This step is also important because many educators don't have the opportunity to engage in this type of reflective work throughout the multiple phases of their careers. While some may encounter it in a required course or professional development training, the reality is that working with people different from yourself means continuously facing new challenges and learning opportunities. Approaching this work with the mindset that each interaction is an opportunity to grow as an educator requires intentionality and a commitment to lifelong learning.

The above exercise is also helpful at the end of a school year or program. What did you learn about yourself? How can you incorporate your learnings into your professional development for the next school year? How can you tailor your own learning around the gaps you have?

Beyond Being "Not Racist"—Toward Active Anti-Racism

In this current climate, the anti-DEI movement has led to policy rollbacks, from higher education institutions eliminating race-conscious admissions to corporations like Target scaling back their DEI initiatives. The loudest voices in the room often belong to those resisting true diversity of the United States, advocating instead for a more homogeneous society. Conversely, on the other side of the spectrum, many individuals claim they are *not racist*. However, this perspective is often rooted in the desire to avoid being perceived as a *bad person*, rather than actively working against racism.

When working with students and families, we need to understand the difference between passive neutrality and active justice. Discussion of race can be uncomfortable because we are all products of a system where racial inequity is a lived reality. These inequities are reinforced by laws and policies that have historically disadvantaged certain groups. The backlash against policies designed to address systemic harm often frames those advocating for racial equity as "always making things about race." However, acknowledging these injustices is necessary for meaningful progress.

Engaging in anti-racist work requires self-reflection, and at times, discomfort. But pushing through that discomfort fosters growth. Becoming an anti-racist educator who actively supports families and students strengthens communities. Our ultimate goal is to center the humanity of our students and their families. By doing so, we become better leaders and create environments where families feel respected, valued, and treated with dignity and compassion. Overcoming racist practices allows students to thrive and reassures families that they have a true partner in their child's education. Even when internal resistance arises, keep moving forward—growth is on the other side.

As you continue to grow, your perspectives will evolve. You will be informed by others' perspectives that will allow you to gain a deeper understanding of different lived experiences. In the context of race, a person from a marginalized racial background experiences many injustices as compared to their white counterparts. Many of these are due to policies and practices related to laws that still have affected us. A recent article published by KFF, also known as the Kaiser Family Foundation, a nonprofit organization that provides health policy research, journalism, and communications, reported that large racial disparities continue to persist. The article stated:

> Maternal and infant health disparities reflect broader underlying social and economic inequities that are rooted in racism and discrimination. Differences in health insurance coverage and access to care play a role in driving worse maternal and infant health outcomes for people of color. However, inequities in broader social and economic factors, including income, are primary drivers for maternal and infant health disparities. Moreover, disparities in maternal and infant health persist even when controlling for certain underlying social and economic factors, such as education and income, pointing to the roles racism and discrimination play in driving disparities. (Hill et al., 2024)

This is how racism functions in healthcare. The treatment of Black people and other people of color within the healthcare system creates an ecosystem of mistrust, where basic healthcare needs are often unmet. Research shows that both Black women and Black children experience disparities in treatment. Similarly, when we consider how Black families are treated in educational and out-of-school program settings, communication emerges as a key area of concern. Understanding cultural norms and expectations is essential. In my own research of parents' experiences during the pandemic, the essential workers in my study were all Black mothers. These mothers expressed frustration for not having open lines of communication with their children's teachers.

Some mothers reported not knowing that their children were falling behind on assignments until final grades were posted on the online platform. In most cases, they wished that someone from school would have simply reached out to them by phone. These mothers expressed frustration over the lack of open communication with their children's teachers. Some mothers reported not knowing that their children were falling behind on assignments until final grades were posted on the online platform. In most cases, they wished that someone from the school had simply reached out to them by phone. In many instances, no one had contacted them at all, highlighting the urgent need for improved communication efforts between schools and Black families.

It is important for educators to acknowledge and address internal resistance and discomfort when working with families of color. Letting go of any preconceived notions, stereotypes, and misconceptions of parents of color is important to having a humanizing relationship and communication. In my experience, I've seen educators who, assuming parents will respond negatively, avoid communicating with them altogether. However, building strong relationships from the start is crucial. Find opportunities to get to know families—invite them into your space, offer food, and create an environment where trust can flourish. Establishing these connections early makes it easier to maintain open lines of communication and foster a positive partnership throughout the year.

Second Prong: Whose Story Is Being Told? (Critical Media and Curriculum Analysis)

The second prong is to ask: *Whose Story Is Being Told?* This step challenges anti-racist practitioners to center the voices and experiences of our most marginalized students. In order to grow as an anti-racist educator, you must critically reflect on representations in the media and curriculum materials. Where there are gaps, it is important to fill those spaces with a full representation of the students you serve, but also of the larger society. While representation is empowering for those who are underrepresented, it is equally important for those outside of those experiences and backgrounds to see the full humanity of those who are not like them. The more we can humanize each other, the less likely we are to create divisions of "us" versus "them."

Examining Representation in Education

In a schooling context, textbooks, books, classroom discussions, and visual materials shape how students understand the world. These elements signal what is important, whose stories matter, and who is valued in society. A study by First Book (2023), a national nonprofit organization dedicated to removing barriers to equitable education for children in low-income communities, identified key findings on this issue:

1. Students' Reading Scores Increased After Educators Added Diverse Books to Their Classroom Libraries.
2. Students Spent More Time Reading After Educators Added Diverse Books to Their Classroom Libraries.
3. Allowing Students to Choose Which Books They Want to Read Positively Affects Outcomes.
4. Educators Believe That Diverse Books are Important, but Diverse Books Are a Small Percentage of Their Classroom Libraries.
5. A Majority of Students Chose to Read Diverse Books That Serve as Mirrors, Where They Can See Themselves. (p. 4)

A diverse set of books benefits students in important ways—they spend more time reading, their reading scores increase, and they see themselves reflected in literature, which boosts self-confidence. One of the most compelling findings, however, relates to educators. Let's take a closer look. As part of their research, First Book conducted pre-surveys to understand educators' perspectives on diverse books and to assess the availability of diverse books in their classroom libraries. Classroom libraries are typically used for free reading time, peer reading, and small group book clubs. We know that the more students read for fun, the more likely they are to engage with reading.

According to the research they did with the pre-surveys:

- 99 percent of educators believed that having a diverse classroom library is important.

- 75 percent of participants reported serving predominantly children of color.
- However, only 58 percent felt their current classroom library adequately reflected their students' identities.
- Despite believing in the importance of diverse books, educators reported that diverse books only represented 28 percent of educators' libraries. (p. 4)

What does this tell us? Most educators in this study serve majority students of color, and they overwhelmingly believe that diverse books are essential. But there's a gap—why aren't these books making it into the classroom? Let me share an experience that sheds light on this issue.

As a university professor, much of my work involves collaborating with local schools. I also run a Freedom School summer program on campus, which uses culturally relevant books to help prevent summer slide. I will share this program further in chapter 4.

Given my role, I am often invited to deliver professional development opportunities for educators. In one particular workshop, I was asked to meet with teachers to discuss how they could better support Black male students. During this workshop, I emphasized the importance of using culturally relevant books in their classes. However, teachers expressed frustration—they weren't sure where to find books for their students from diverse backgrounds. This highlighted a crucial issue: Educators must be intentional about ant-racist practices and disrupting the status quo. Committing to anti-racism in education means actively seeking out professional development opportunities beyond what our employers provide. It also means rethinking how we select books, discussion, and materials—ensuring that dominant narratives do not erase the voices and experiences of marginalized communities.

Deconstructing the Dominant Narrative

By providing diverse materials to the students and families you work with, you can humanize underrepresented voices and validate their lived experiences. Inclusion fosters a deeper understanding of communities and their members by allowing multiple perspectives at the table. However, when we focus on only one narrative or a single story, we replicate harm and perpetuate stereotypes. When these stereotypes are the only representations of people, they limit the ability to imagine alternative narratives and more nuanced truths.

Take, for example, a persistent stereotype—the idea that Black people are lazy. This harmful trope has been reinforced through Blackface performance, TV characters, and literature. Even some of the most iconic civil rights stories have been oversimplified in ways that distort reality. If you ask a school-aged child, "Who was Rosa Parks?" they might respond, "She was a tired Black woman who was so tired that day she refused to get up to give her seat to a white person." This framing reduces her to being tired and lazy, implying that exhaustion, rather than resistance, was at the core of her actions.

This narrative erases the broader context of racial injustice. It omits the fact that Black people were subjected to daily dehumanization—forced to move their seats further and further back whenever a white person boarded. They were also charged higher fares to board the same bus. Historian Jean Theoharris, in her book titled *The Rebellious Life of Mrs. Rosa Parks*, offers a more complete and humanizing perspective. Parks was not just a tired woman—she was a lifelong activist committed to voting rights, anti-apartheid movements, reparations, fair housing, women's rights, and the fight against police violence.

For educators seeking lesson plans and resources that accurately portray her activism, The Zinn Education Project is an excellent resource. This organization promotes teaching history through multiple perspectives offering webinars, lesson plans, and other resources dedicated to supporting teaching multiple perspectives. When considering stories like Rosa Parks's, it is also important to apply the lens of *Intersectionality*, a term coined by legal expert Kimberlé Crenshaw. According to Encyclopedia Britannica (Samie, 2024), intersectionality refers to the interaction and cumulative effects of multiple forms of discrimination affecting the daily lives of individuals, particularly women of color. In storytelling, we must examine not just race, but also gender, class, and other intersecting forms of oppression. Only then can we ensure that the stories we tell do justice to the people who lived them.

Application to Teaching Practice

When evaluating the materials and resources you provide in educational spaces, it is critical to assess them for bias. The goal is to ensure that materials reflect a variety of voices, experiences, and backgrounds rather than reinforcing a single dominant narrative. Tools for analyzing bias in curricula and materials can help educators create inclusive learning environments. At the end of this chapter, I have provided several tools and rubrics to assist in assessing bias in your curriculum. One valuable resource is The Comprehensive Center Network Region 8, MDE *Tools and Guidance for Evaluating Bias in Instructional Materials* (Coomer et al., 2017).

Third Prong: How Is the Story Being Told and Who Benefits?

Understanding Power in Narrative Construction

Storytelling has the power to be both transformative and harmful. It allows us to understand others' lived experiences, fostering empathy and expanding our worldview. However, the way a story is told and by whom shapes what we understand about the people and events involved. Take, for example, the story of Indigenous youth and Indian boarding schools. The widely accepted narrative has often portrayed these schools as institutions meant to "assimilate" Indigenous children into white/European culture. The storytellers—those in positions of power—crafted a version of history that suggested these schools were necessary, that Indigenous people were unfit to raise their children, and that removing them from families was somehow better in their best interest.

> I know that this process will be long and difficult. I know that this process will be painful. It won't undo the heartbreak and loss we feel. But only by acknowledging the past can we work toward a future that we're all proud to embrace.
>
> —Secretary Deb Haaland

In 2021, Secretary of the Interior Deb Haaland at the National Congress of American Indians 2021 Mid-Year Conference addressed the audience and introduced the Federal Indian Boarding School Initiative. This initiative would include a comprehensive review of the highly troubling federal boarding school policies. When we consider the story of Indigenous people in our society, we see a narrative shaped by misinformation, omissions, and outright falsehoods. These inaccuracies have contributed to systemic struggles within Indigenous communities, reinforcing harmful stereotypes and erasing historical truths. The distorted narrative has been represented in history textbooks, the romanticized story of Thanksgiving and media portrayals—from sports mascots to glorified depictions of the "Wild West" in films. It took years of activism, protests, and demands from Indigenous communities before the National Football League's Washington, D.C. team finally changed its racist mascot name. By challenging these narratives and centering Indigenous voices and histories, we can begin to correct the record and move toward true representation and justice.

Reframing Narratives for Justice

To be an anti-racist educator, we need to continually shift our language from deficit-based to asset-based framing of marginalized communities. To do this, we need to spend time with marginalized communities and allow them to share their stories. We must also encourage and create opportunities for students who are not members of marginalized communities to critically analyze the stories they consume. This means fostering responsibility in questioning representations, recognizing biases, and understanding how media and historical narratives often misalign with the lived experiences of the communities they claim to portray. In addition, we must connect curriculum to students' lives by implementing culturally responsive teaching that makes learning relevant and meaningful. This includes centering student experiences as valid sources of knowledge, ensuring that their voices and perspectives are actively engaged in the learning process.

Fourth Prong: Taking Action for Humanity

To truly embody anti-racist education, taking action is essential. This is the most important step of the framework. Traditional views of educators often emphasize a one-directional approach—walking into a classroom of afterschool space, delivering information, and considering the job done. However, culturally responsive teaching has already pushed us forward by emphasizing the importance of meaningful relationships with students and their families. What I propose is that we go even further—toward active advocacy. Educators hold a tremendous amount of power when it comes to shaping school policies and school culture. That same power should be leveraged to dismantle systemic racism and promote equity in education. Moving beyond awareness means taking deliberate steps to challenge inequities, advocate for students and families, and transform our learning environments into spaces of justice and empowerment.

Beyond the Classroom: Educators as Community Advocates

Educators play a critical role in shaping policies, school culture, and advocacy efforts—especially in an era where publicly funded educational opportunities for youth and their families are under threat. It is essential that educators see themselves as community advocates with the power to drive meaningful change. One key avenue for advocacy is joining the national organizations that focus on education, equity, and youth development. Some examples include:

- National Education Association
- The Children's Defense Fund (CDF)
- The Council for Opportunity in Education
- National Parent Teacher Association

- National Network for Youth
- Council for Exceptional Children

Remaining connected to national advocacy groups allows educators to stay informed about policy changes that may affect students and families at the local level. Many of these organizations host advocacy days, where members visit state and US capitals to meet with lawmakers, highlighting the importance of education programming and advocating for funding support.

To build stronger solidarity, educators should also encourage families to join these organizations. When families actively participate in advocacy, they gain opportunities to make their voices heard and shape policies that directly affect their children's education and well-being. Empowering families as advocates ensures that decision-makers hear firsthand what matters most to the communities they serve.

Challenging Systemic Injustices in Schools

Local advocacy is essential for addressing inequitable funding, discipline disparities, and access to resources. As an educator, this means actively participating in school board meetings and engaging with local representatives such as your city council members. By sharing the importance of your program and the impact it has made on the community, you can advocate for funding to support those programs. Additionally, involvement with school boards can help expand out-of-school programming, as these governing bodies are invested in supporting youth development. In my own work, I have collaborated with a local community group to establish a free summer program called CDF Freedom Schools. By bringing all stakeholders together, we have been able to create a culturally responsive curriculum that enriches the city's most marginalized youth. By bringing all stakeholders together, we have been able to create a culturally responsive curriculum that enriches the city's most marginalized youth. This model demonstrates that when educators, policymakers, and community leaders invest in students collectively, we can break cycles of educational inequity and foster meaningful change.

The Role of Media and Misinformation in Shaping Bias

In today's information age, we have constant access to information through social media streaming platforms and online videos. However, the regulation of online content remains minimal, allowing misinformation and harmful narratives to spread unchecked. In January 2025, Facebook CEO, Mark Zuckerberg, announced that Meta would no longer use third-party fact-checking programs and instead implement community notes, like those used on X (formerly Twitter) platform. In a video statement Mr. Zuckerberg stated: "We're going to get back to our roots and focus on reducing mistakes, simplifying our policies and restoring free expression on our platforms." While this shift is framed as an effort to promote free expression, it also raises concerns about increased misinformation and the potential harm of unchecked narratives. Many of these harmful images and messages reinforce stereotypes, racism, homophobia, and xenophobia, further distancing educators from their students and families and eroding our shared humanity.

As anti-racist educators and practitioners, we must critically reflect on the information we consume and challenge our own biases. Doing this work requires ongoing commitment, not just a one-time professional development session. It is a long-term journey that demands continuous self-reflection, learning, and action to create truly inclusive and just educational spaces.

The Neuroscience of Bias and Changing Mindsets

When we encounter someone different from us, our brains automatically begin a sorting process, known as "ingroup bias" and "outgroup bias." Over time, repeated exposure to societal messages about which groups are "safe" or "harmful" reinforces these biases. Our brains continuously seek a sense of belonging, sorting people into categories based on race, gender, sports teams, school affiliations, and more. In the context of professional development for educators, many opportunities are top-down initiatives, with topics selected by employers rather than by individual choice. These sessions might include online training, expert-led workshops, or book clubs. However, the timing of these opportunities often conflicts with other professional demands, leading participants to mentally check out—preoccupied with their growing to-do lists rather than fully engaging with the material.

What many well-being coaches and cognitive researchers suggest is that true, ongoing learning requires rewiring how our brains function. The good news? Our brains are highly adaptable thanks to neuroplasticity, which allows us to change our thoughts and behaviors over time. Neuroplasticity operates in two key ways:

- Experience-Dependent Neuroplasticity: This process involves automatic, unconscious habits formed through repeated behaviors, whether helpful or harmful.
- Self-Directed Neuroplasticity: This occurs when we intentionally reshape our thoughts and actions through deliberate effort.

Recognizing these processes is critical for personal growth. If we want to move beyond ingrained biases, we must actively work to disrupt old patterns and build new, more inclusive ways of thinking.

Conclusion: Doing the Work Is a Lifelong Commitment

Educators must recognize that being an anti-racist educator is a continuous journey, not a final destination. This work is never truly "finished"—it is an evolving process and commitment. A commitment to this work means a commitment to justice through ongoing reflection, readings, attending events, and joining community organizations committed to racial justice. It requires stepping outside of comfort zones and actively working to dismantle systemic inequities. Becoming an anti-racist educator doesn't just benefit you—it transforms the students and families you serve, creating stronger, more inclusive communities in the process.

Emphasizing the Journey, Not the Destination

Anti-racist work is never "finished"—it is a lifelong commitment. It means calling out and calling in. Calling out racial injustice means naming it directly using phrases like: "I noticed," "I'm curious," and "I believe." These statements invite dialogue rather than defensiveness. Calling in means creating space for reflection, accountability, and repair—allowing individuals or institutions to address and correct harm. Being an anti-racist educator means embracing continuous learning: learning from families' lived experiences, learning from communities, and learning from experts, research, and ongoing conversations. Above all, anti-racism is not just a practice—it is an identity. It means showing up every day with the commitment to dismantling inequities, amplifying marginalized voices, and fostering justice in every space you enter.

Call to Action: How Will You Commit to Reflection for Humanity?

As we began this chapter with writing, let's also end with writing. Reflection is essential in your journey toward becoming an anti-racist educator. Below are a few reflection prompts to help guide your ongoing learning and commitment:

Community Engagement

- Where can I learn more about my local community?
- What organizations support communities of color (Black, African American, Hispanic/Latino/a, Indigenous, and Asian American)?
- Do these organizations host public events I can attend or support?

Representation and Inclusion in My Organization

- How can I amplify more diverse voices in my workplace?
- What opportunities can I create for people of color to share their experiences, cultures, and perspectives?

Advocacy and Support

- How can I be a stronger advocate for people of color in my organization?
- In what ways can I support students and families of color to ensure they feel valued, respected, and included?

Expanding My Knowledge

- What books, documentaries, or podcasts can I engage with to deepen my understanding of racial justice and lived experiences of communities of color?

Meaningful Interactions

- Where in my personal life can I build genuine, intentional connections with people of color?
- Can I do this through my faith community, volunteering, or local events?

Reflection leads to action. Take time to engage with these questions and commit to tangible steps toward a more inclusive and just world.

Final Thought: A Community Effort for Collective Liberation

As we close this chapter, let's reflect on the power of one individual committed to justice. Imagine the impact if people in communities across the nation dedicated themselves to racial justice and anti-racist practices. When individuals come together in solidarity, their collective efforts create lasting change—centering humanity, by seeing the humanity of the families and children they have the privilege of serving. This kind of commitment doesn't just benefit individuals; it transforms entire communities. A society rooted in anti-racism and equity fosters an environment where everyone can thrive. When we create spaces where all people—especially youth and families—are valued, respected, and empowered, we move closer to true liberation.

Justice is not just an ideal—it's an action. And with each step, we contribute to a better, more just world.

List of Resources

1. Assessing Bias in Standards and Curricular Materials—Created by: Midwest and Plains Equity Assistance Center (Coomer et al., February 2017), https://files.eric.ed.gov/fulltext/ED623049.pdf
2. Tools and Guidance for Evaluating Bias in Instructional Materials—Created by The Comprehensive Center Network Region 8, https://www.michigan.gov/-/media/Project/Websites/mde/Academic-Standards/Tools_Guidance_Eval_Bias_Instructional_Mats.pdf?rev=1cc5205c9d8a4911b1cb5d7905882727
3. 2023 Culturally Responsive ELA Curriculum Scorecard—Created by NYC Coalition for Educational Justice, The Metropolitan Center for Research on Equity and the Transformation of Schools, https://steinhardt.nyu.edu/metrocenter/ejroc/services/culturally-responsive-curriculum-scorecards
4. Washington Models for the Evaluation of Bias Content in Instructional Materials, https://oercommons.org/courseware/lesson/68056/overview (Newfarmer, M., Soots, B., & Simmons, M., 2009).

5. Evaluating American Indian Materials and Resources for the Classroom, revised and updated by Laura Ferguson, original version compiled by Dr. Murton McCluskey, 1992. Montana Office of Public Instruction, 2015, https://opi.mt.gov/Portals/182/Page%20Files/Indian%20Education/Indian%20Education%20101/Evaluating%20AI%20Materials%20and%20Resources%20for%20the%20Classroom.pdf

References

Coomer, M. N., S. M. Skelton, T. S. Kyser, C. Warren, and K. A. K. Thorius (2017). *Assessing Bias in Standards and Curricular Materials: Equity Tool*. Great Lakes Equity Center.

First Book. (2023). *The Impact of a Diverse Classroom Library*. https://firstbook.org/wp-content/uploads/2023/09/2023-Impact-of-a-Diverse-Classroom-Library-FINAL-9-6-23.pdf.

Hill, R., A. Rao, S. Artiga, and U. Ranji (2024). *Racial Disparities in Maternal and Infant Health: Current Status and Efforts to Address Them*. Kaiser Family Foundation. https://www.kff.org/racial-equity-and-health-policy/issue-brief/racial-disparities-in-maternal-and-infant-health-current-status-and-efforts-to-address-them/.

McCluskey, M. (Writer), and L. Ferguson (Reviser). (2015). *Evaluating American Indian Materials and Resources for the Classroom*. Montana Office of Public Instruction.

Samie, A. (2024, December 20). *Intersectionality. Encyclopedia Britannica.* https://www.britannica.com/topic/intersectionality.

Newfarmer, M., Soots, B., and Simmons, M. (2009). *Washington Models for the Evaluation of Bias Content in Instructional Materials*. Retrieved from https://oercommons.org/courseware/lesson/68056/overview

Our analysis of funds of knowledge represents a positive (and, we argue, realistic) view of households as containing ample cultural and cognitive resources with great potential utility for classroom instruction.... This view of households, we should mention, contrasts sharply with prevailing views of working-class families as disorganized socially and deficient intellectually.
                            Moll, L. C., Amanti, C., Neff, D., & González, N. (1992)

Introduction

This chapter explores data I have collected over the years, highlighting the ways Black families have consistently asked educators to recognize their full humanity. The persistent narrative that Black families don't care or are not involved has had a long history in public debate of parent involvement. My research focuses on three key areas: school-based mentoring, out-of-school educational programs, and online learning during the pandemic. Mentoring has been positioned as a tool to improve student outcomes, with white mentors frequently paired with Black youth to support academic performance, cultural enrichment, and college enrollment. However, my research reveals that many Black parents are left out of the mentoring relationship, despite their desire to be active participants.

    Additionally, my findings show that Black families intentionally seek educational opportunities that affirm cultural identity and provide uplift—filling critical gaps left by the public educational system. Furthermore, my research on the experiences of Black parents during e-learning in the pandemic sheds light on the lack of compassion they encountered and their hopes for a more supportive educational environment. Finally, this chapter will explore the role of out-of-school programming in supporting Black families, with a specific focus on my work with the CDF's Freedom Schools program. This initiative is designed to combat summer slide by enhancing reading literacy, parent engagement, and civic development.

The chapter will present research findings and challenge educators to recognize that students do not live in isolation I from the families and caregivers. In fact, these families actively leverage the resources available to them to enhance their children's educational opportunities and mitigate the harm caused by racist educational practices and systems. Additionally, this chapter will provide practical strategies for educators to foster meaningful relationships with families and create opportunities for open, humanity-centered communication. But what does it mean to center humanity?

According to Merriam-Webster, the definition of *humanity* is the totality of human beings. This perspective urges educators to see students as full, complex individuals—acknowledging not just their academic identities but their lived experiences, emotions, and relationships. When we look at our students, do we see them the same as other children in our lives, such as our kids, nieces, nephews, cousins, and neighbors? Kids with the same curiosity, clumsiness, laughter, joy, and love? If we follow in the footsteps of the business world, they use a term called *human-centered design*. A Harvard Business School Online Blog, entitled *What Is Human-Centered Design?*, describes a model that prioritizes people in the development of products and services. According to the author, "Human-centered design is a problem-solving technique that puts real people at the center of the development process, enabling you to create products and services that resonate and are tailored to your audience's needs" (Landry, 2020).

This idea of prioritizing humanity is not new. During the Civil Rights Movement, when leaders fought for social integration, Dr. King concluded one of his speeches with a powerful call to action, reminding us that the fight for justice must be rooted in recognizing and affirming the full humanity of every child. He stated: "Make a career of humanity. Commit yourself to the noble struggle for equal rights. You will make a better person of yourself, a greater nation of your country, and a finer world to live in" (National Park Service, 2024).

The goal is to embrace the full complexity of what it means to be human and the challenges individuals face in their daily lives. It is easy to find ourselves in discord with parents, especially the most marginalized members of society. Often, the most vocal parents are unfairly labeled as "difficult," when in reality, their advocacy stems from a deep desire to secure the best opportunities for their children. However, we shift our gaze to understand that most parents simply want the best for their children. Many Black parents have navigated educational systems that are hostile, racist, underfunded, and marked by systemic racism—leaving them underrepresented and underserved. These lived experiences shape their concerns and anxieties when sending their children to school.

By shifting our perspective, we can move beyond judgment and instead prioritize meaningful collaboration with families. When we listen to their wishes for their children and center their humanity, we create environments where families can truly thrive. In doing so, we cultivate spaces where young people not only see themselves reflected in the world but also recognize their own limitless potential. Ultimately, when we uplift and support our youth, all of society benefits—allowing brilliance to shine in its fullest form.

Lastly, the chapter opens with a quote from Moll et al. (1992), whose work challenges long-standing narratives that frame Latino working-class families as lacking in an educational environment. Instead, their research emphasizes the importance of teaching educators to utilize qualitative research methods and ethnographic approaches to better understand their students' households and bridge the gap between school and community. This reframing positions working families as experts in their own experiences and encourages educators to adopt the role of researchers—learning from the communities they serve rather than imposing external assumptions. This perspective serves as the foundation for this chapter. Below, you will find an exploration of the historical context of parent engagement, particularly in relation to Black families.

To fully understand the challenges of parental involvement, especially in Black communities, we need to examine the historical narratives around Black parents and their lack of engagement. Decades of research have demonstrated that parental involvement improves academic outcomes for students. However, the ways in which parents engage—and how that is perceived—vary significantly. When focusing on African/American and Latino/Hispanic students, families in these communities have often been judged for not being "involved" enough. Lack of involvement is usually portrayed as not attending events during the school day or missing Parent Teacher conferences. However, the stereotype of disengaged parents has deep historical roots.

A pivotal national discourse emerged with the 1965 publication of *The Negro Family: The Case for National Action*, also known as the Moynihan report, named for its author Daniel Patrick Moynihan. Moynihan was a sociologist and staffer in the Johnson administration. The report was preceded by Johnson's War on Poverty, the government's first attempt to address poverty within the Black community on a national level. The Moynihan report has been viewed as controversial in its key argument—Black family problems are traced to the lack of married couples. The report states, "The fundamental problem in which this is most clearly the case, is that of family structure. The evidence not final, but powerfully persuasive—is that the Negro family in the urban ghettos is crumbling" (Moynihan,1965, p. 4). Moynihan, who wrote the report, at the time was the Assistant Secretary of Labor. His effort to write the report was an attempt to get the Johnson White House to be convinced that Civil Rights legislation alone would not lead to racial equity. The report led to debates weather polices could lead to race-based economic equality conversely conservative thought believed the report on inequality helped their argument, that only through racial self-help could the structure of the Black family be changed.

School-Based Mentoring and Black Families

School-based mentoring has become a widely used tool for supporting students, especially those from marginalized communities, in achieving academic success. My research examines how parents utilize school-based mentoring to support their children. Early research studies indicated that parents should not be involved in mentoring relationships. For example, Miller (2007), detailing best practice principles for formal youth mentoring relationships, urges programs to "seek the support of parents/careers" but "not their active engagement in the mentoring process," as "non-supportive parents can sabotage the mentor–protégé´ relationship" (p. 318). Similarly, Keller (2005) proposed that mentoring relationships should be within family and agency contexts; however, this model has not been tested empirically. Consequently, families are not understood to be part of the mentoring relationship.

Some studies suggest that parent involvement can present complications from the mentor's perspective. Styles and Morrow (1992), in a qualitative study of mentoring relationships, identified issues associated with parents, which include miscommunication between mentors and parents, parents including mentors in family disputes, and parents' attempts to influence the mentoring relationships. While this research includes parents, the research is limited as conducted and reported from the perspective of the mentor. Parents have received little investigation in the mentoring literature, yet it is clear that they have much to bring to the relationship.

Spencer et al. (2011) identified ways parents can help support mentoring relationships and make them stronger. These include sharing thier hopes and expectations for mentoring relationships, establishing trust with the imentor, creating support for the mentoring relationship, and, most importantly, sharing reflections on and experiences with cultural differences being experienced between child and mentor. Despite these contributions, parental perspectives remain largely absent from mentoring research.

I argue that mentoring alone cannot change the ways in which inequality affects youths of color. It is this very inequality that Black mothers recognize and aim to disrupt by taking advantage of programs that report that their children will be successful if they participate. The mothers, who often navigate the waters of racism, poverty, and limited opportunities, operate with what DuBois (2008) termed *double consciousness*. They are acutely aware of their position within a white supremacist society yet remain determined to create pathways for their children's success. For these mothers, success is defined by milestones such as graduating from high school, attending college, and obtaining a job.

At the center of this project is the impact of mentoring programing on Black mothers. Youth mentoring programs are not designed for mothers; however, I would suggest that the experiences of mothers of color are important as their experiences have a direct impact on the lives of their children. This work is grounded to Black feminist thought (Hill Collins, 2009) which is defined below:

> For African American women, critical social theory encompasses bodies of knowledge and a set of institutional practices that actively grapple with central questions facing the US Black women as a group remain oppressed within a US context characterized by injustice. This neither means that all of African American women within the group are oppressed in the same way, nor that some US Black women do not suppress others. Black feminist thought's identity as "critical" social theory lies in its commitment to justice, both for US Black women as a collectivity and for that of other similarly oppressed groups. (p. 12)

Briggs (1998) suggested that social capital involves connections to a system of human relationships, to accomplish things that matter to us and solve everyday problems.

This concept of social capital takes place in two forms (Dominguez & Watkins, 2003):

1. Social leverage: social capital that helps one "get ahead" or change one's opportunity set through access to job information, say, or a recommendation for a scholarship or loan.
2. Social support: social capital that helps one "get by" or cope. This might include being able to get a ride, confide in someone, or obtain a small cash loan in an emergency. (p. 113)

While Black feminist thought guides the motivation for undertaking this work, I find the work of Briggs (1998) and Dominguez and Watkins (2003) useful contributions to the conceptual framework of this project. The crux of this project is to understand ways in which Black mothers generate social capital at the individual level.

To understand the role of mentoring in Black families, I aimed to answer the following research questions:

1. What roles do Black parents play in mentoring relationships?
2. What are parents' perspectives on mentoring, mentors, and the mentoring program?

3. What aspects of this school-based mentoring program contributed to its sustained relationship with parents?
4. How is social capital implicated in the parents' relation to the mentoring program?
5. What are the implications of the relationships for the future of school-based mentoring?

To contextualize this research, it is important to understand the demographic and economic landscape of the school district where the school-based mentoring program was implemented. According to 2023 US Census data, the town (which I call Addison) has a population of some 62,000. The racial demographics breaks down to 66.7 percent white, 10.9 percent Black, 0.6 percent American Indian, and 13.2 percent Asian. In terms of economic indicators, homeownership in Addison stands at 48.7 percent of folks who own a home with a median home of $576,500. The median gross rental rate is $1,483. The median household income is $85,825. Despite these figures, 19.6 percent of people live below the poverty level. Additionally, households with a computer in 2019–2023 was 99 percent. Currently, Addison public schools and the district spend about $8,155.09 per student, as compared to the state which spends $7,115.73 per pupil and the Federal government spends $890.48 per student in this district. According to North Carolina Department of Public Instruction data, the performance of each student group on the ABCs end-of-grade tests indicates that 95 percent of white students, 61.3 percent of Hispanic students, and 53.3 percent of Black students passed both the reading and math tests. In the state, schools that are designated as Honor Schools of Excellence have at least 90 percent of students at grade level and the school made expected growth or more and met all Annual Measurable Objectives (AMOs). Addison's school district has a 4-Year cohort graduation rate of 94.8 percent, reflecting a strong overall performance yet underscoring the persistent racial achievement gap within the district.

On the surface, this school district appears to be thriving, consistently ranking among the top-performing districts in the country. It has been ranked in the top 100 of American public high schools according to the *U.S.News & World Report*. Additionally, it was considered one of America's best high schools according to *Newsweek*. The school district is known for its exemplary academic standards. However, when it comes to the academic achievement of the Black students, the story is quite different. Black students in the district have lower graduation rates; among Black students attending Riverbank High, 78.8 percent of Black ninth graders graduated from high school four years later, as compared to 91.4 percent of white students. Among Black students attending Pinewood High School, 82 percent graduated four years later, as compared to 94.4 percent of white students (see appendix A).

The mentoring program was established in response to growing concerns about the opportunity gap, more commonly referred to as the achievement gap among Black students. Local newspapers documented the turmoil in the town starting in 1996, when one of the articles highlighted the frustration of the local teachers for feeling the blame of the lack of performance by Black students. The frustration extended to the school's principal, who, according to the local newspaper, acknowledged that Black students at Riverbank High had not shown significant improvement since he started working there. He further noted that faculty members largely opposed initiatives aimed at supporting Black students, and rarely attended meetings designed to address their needs.

Amid these racial tensions and concerns over the Black-white achievement gap, the Gold Medal Mentoring Program was developed. This district-wide student support initiative was designed to improve academic achievement among African American and Latino students by fostering success across multiple developmental areas.

History of Youth Mentoring

The emergence of mentoring in social service programs can be traced back to the Workforce Investment Act of 1998 (Walker, 2005). As private businesses increasingly promoted mentoring throughout the early 1990s, interest in one-on-one mentoring programs expanded, gaining traction through media exposure (Walker, 2005). Freedman (1999) advocated for youth mentoring not only as a means to support young people but also as a way to sustain a culture of volunteerism. He argued:

> A second reason for maintaining volunteer involvement is mentoring's potential for meeting important needs of adults, who can benefit themselves from the mentoring interaction, through satisfying a sense of generativity. Mentoring is a reciprocal relationship. (p. 125)

Freedman's perspective highlights the dual benefits of mentoring, where both the mentor and mentees experience personal growth and fulfillment.

Youth mentoring also reached the attention of President Clinton, who said,

> Most Americans are not for "big government"; they are for volunteerism and the "personal touch" versus the paid professional in helping people; and prefer to think most individual issues can be resolved by willpower and determination, with a minimum of outside help, rather than by the provision of comprehensive services. (as quoted in DuBois and Karcher, 2005, p. 510)

At this juncture, the emergence of free programming to address the needs of minority and low-income youths intersects with broader welfare reform efforts. While the early 1990s witnessed a huge surge in youth mentoring, particularly as a social capital investment, contemporary youth mentoring efforts have increasingly been positioned as a way to improve academic achievement.

Numerous studies have sought to understand the mechanisms through which mentoring operates. Much of the literature focuses on mentoring relationships, their benefits, and the dynamics of the school-based mentoring programs. The growth of school-based mentoring can be attributed to the belief that mentoring can improve academic achievement in this area of high-stakes testing. However, in thinking about school-based mentoring, it is important to note the complicated relationship between schools and youths of color. For youths of color, the discourse around academic achievement often has not led to one clear solution. One area of focus has been on teaching and teachers. Rong (1996) asserted, "How teachers perceive students is affected by their own race and gender as are teachers' attitudes and behaviors toward students of different racial groups" (p. 284). Rong further stated that the "teaching profession is becoming less ethnically diverse and less able to function effectively for the culturally and ethnically diversified schools in U.S. society" (pp. 284–5).

While research has explored teacher preparedness, studies suggest that students perform better in classrooms where teachers implement culturally relevant or responsive pedagogical methods. Two main theories are relevant to incorporating culturally sensitive pedagogies: culturally responsive teaching and culturally relevant pedagogy (CRP). Additionally, prior scholarship by Briggs (1998) and Dominguez and Watkins (2003) on social capital offer a useful framework for understanding how mothers utilize mentoring as a strategy to support their children's educational success. Dominguez and Watkins found that

> ties offer a viable and important alternative when friendship and family-based networks are unavailable or ineffective. Although social support is most often associated with "strong ties" we saw several examples of women receiving food, childcare, jobs and even emotional support from social service providers who are in essence "weak ties." (p. 121)

Their argument suggests that when family and friend networks are unavailable, the women in the study relied on institution-based networks for support. Their work fills an important gap, as prior analyses of social support networks have often excluded professional and institution-based relationships. This perspective is particularly useful in framing the first major theme that emerged from my data analysis. Building on Briggs' work, I have identified this first theme as *social support*.

Mentoring Role for Parents

In this case, the mothers enrolled their children in the mentoring program to take advantage of the social support the school-based mentoring program offered. There were clear strategies within the mentoring relationship that the mothers demonstrate in utilizing the mentoring program. They were generating social capital through ties that offered social support or social leverage. By enrolling in the mentoring program, this research reveals two key mobility strategies used by these mothers: (a) developing a social support network and (b) creating social leverage.

Understanding the systematic racial injustices Black mothers navigate in schools highlights how they strategically leverage available resources to fill critical gaps. My study further found that the mentoring relationship yields an opportunity for leverage. This leverage, I would argue, involves mothers generating social capital under the contingencies of systemic racial oppression in the school system and society. The desire, here often described by the mothers as Black male mentorship, academic support, and exposure to cultural and social outings, is an expression of what they see as needed to navigate white supremacy.

One respondent shared an incident involving her son and his teachers. She recalled an incident in which her son was disciplined at school following a dispute with a teacher. However, school officials never informed her—nor did her child. It was only after she found the notice in her son's book bag that she was alerted to the situation. The mother described the situation:

> Because his attitude is he gets pissed off at his teacher, they kick him out of class. They had a police officer come and get him out of class. Yeah. It was a mess.... He got cussed out. The teacher admitted. He said he was having a bad day. We had to meet with the teacher. Yeah. The teacher admitted it. He said he was having a bad day, he apologized, said it was out of character for him.

After learning of the incident, the mother decided to take action to make her concerns known:

> I called the principal, assistant principal and told 'em my concerns. I said, "Y'all tried to hide this and it's not gonna go further." So I met with the superintendent, and it went there. I went to the superintendent. At first they gave me the runaround. I had to move the meeting with the superintendent.

The mother actively advocated for her son, expressing deep frustration over the teacher's actions. The parent revealed during the interview that her son's teacher had a history of altercations with students. This mother was more frustrated with the school system and their response. She believed that school administrators did not protect her son:

> And you called to have my son escorted out of school? So I'm still hurt by that. Nobody protected my son, and they swept that under the rug. And had I not found that disciplinary notice, I would have never known.

Another mother shared her experiences with a teacher:

> But see, in the second grade, a teacher told Josh that he would never be anybody, that he would never read or write, um, he probably sells drugs on the street. And she actually told me to my face that she actually felt sorry for me at home. And that's when I told them that they needed to take the child out of the room right now, so I had to clean up a little bit of stuff and let her know that my day on Saturday started before she got up out of the bed, that you know, he was in swimming classes, he was doing basketball, and we go to church on Sunday, so don't tell me that he can't sit still. So don't tell me what he going to be, 'cause you don't know what the future holds.

The mothers also demonstrated that even though they were frustrated with some of the schooling experiences, they did not acquiesce to the system. They turned to advocating for their children. In many circumstances, the mothers understood the context of how Black boys are treated in the school district:

> I advocate for my child. I attend all those IEP meetings because I know about special education—that's what I worked in when I worked in the school system. And you know, being that he's a Black child, Black boy, I know how they try to put our kids in special ed and you know, from my older son, when we was in Addison County schools, it was just a mess, and you know, I vowed that I'm not going to let that happen to my boys. You know, you put my boys in special ed and they always have that label. I refuse to let that happen. You know, I wish other parents would know what it details when your child is in special ed and I feel like somebody

should explain it to them a little more than what they get from the teachers because some of them just really don't know.

Another mother shared her experience of working in the school district and the ways in which race played out:

> Yeah. But when the Black kids did it, it was a big issue. They wanted everything to be mailed out; they wanted the parent was notified right then and there. It was not sweeping up anything under the rug. So that experience, it taught me a valuable experience of how to handle my son in Addison schools—so I said I'm gonna be an advocate for my son, I'm gonna be very supportive of my son and my daughter because I see how Addison schools do this. If you're not a supportive parent, they will tear your child apart. And that's the truth. If you don't support your child, advocate for your child, they will tear your child apart. I am serious.

In addition to their critique of the school system, the mothers also believed that mentoring required a level of commitment from those who choose to participate. They strongly believed that mentoring was a serious responsibility—one that should not be taken lightly. If a mentor was unable to fully commit to the role, the mothers felt it would be better for them not to sign up at all rather than provide inconsistent support:

> And so they will commit to being a mentor but then during the time reality is they don't have the time to actually be a mentor, so the kid don't get to see them as much as you would like them to see 'em.

This narrative surfaced repeatedly in my research. Many mothers expressed disappointment when mentors started strong in the program but later became inconsistent. As one mother put it, "So now, the only downfall with the program is sometimes you can get a mentor who doesn't realize how busy they are."

Much of the concern from the mothers stemmed from their deep desire to protect their children. This finding highlights the need for further research into how parents—particularly Black parents—have been marginalized by school systems and a racialized society. At the same time, it underscores how these same parents are active agents in addressing the oppression they and their children experience.

My understanding of the program was also shaped by interactions with an African American staff member. Many of our conversations revolved around the local school district and community. Through these discussions, I gained deeper insight into the historical and social context of the area and the mentoring program—particularly from the perspective of an African American woman.

I also conducted interviews with mentors in the program. Many mentors described how they came to mentoring as an opportunity to "re-parent" and/or to practice parenting. They often saw themselves as parental figures for the youth they mentored. The interviews raised important questions: Did parents view mentors as a secondary parental figure in their children's lives? Or did mentors perceive themselves as second parents because they believed the child's parents were not meeting certain expectations? Later, as I interviewed parents, their voices reflected a deep concern for their children and a commitment to doing the very best they could. Their narratives made it clear that, despite systemic barriers, they were actively working to support their children's success.

Implications for Mentoring Programs

Understanding why families utilize mentoring programs is crucial before implementing any services. Recognizing that families may come from working-class backgrounds or have lower levels of formal education than their child's mentor does not mean they lack a clear vision for their involvement. Moving beyond dated ideas of parental engagement in mentoring should be a current priority. This requires having early conversations with families to understand their expectations and desires for their child's mentoring experience.

In cross-race mentoring, it is especially important to create opportunities for non-Black mentors to develop a deeper understanding of how race shapes the lives of their mentees as well as the experiences of the parents and caregivers. This means acknowledging the ways in which systemic racism impacts Black families' daily lives—whether in education, health care, or broader societal narratives that are often steeped in misinformation and bias. Because mentoring is frequently positioned as a supplement to educational attainment, the inclusion of parents and caregivers remains essential. Future research should build upon the lessons of this study, particularly by examining the role of schooling experiences as central to the reason parents seek out mentoring programs.

Similarly, existing mentoring programs tend to narrowly define themselves as a social service designed to support children in need. However, this study suggests that mentoring programs should also be understood as sites of possibility—spaces where meaningful relationships, cultural affirmation, and racial identity development can take place. Mentoring is far more than just an adult–child pairing; to fully grasp both its benefits and limitations, we must broaden our perspective and explore its potential expansively. Relatedly, I encourage future research to examine the varied and significant ways parents actively engage in the mentoring process—and how programs can intentionally incorporate parental involvement as a core component of their structure and mission.

Out-of-School Educational Programs: A Response to Systemic Gaps

Given the educational disparities faced by Black youth, many Black parents actively seek enrichment opportunities that affirm their children's cultural identity and support their academic growth. As diversity, equity and inclusion come under increasing scrutiny in public education, families are turning to alternative programs that enhance their children's understanding of cultural values, history, and community engagement. These opportunities have expanded in recent years to include book clubs that focus on diverse literature not only for students from marginalized communities but also for white families to broaden their children's cultural knowledge.

Faith communities have also been a source of cultural affirmation for Black families. Historically, these communities have provided opportunities for youth to celebrate their heritage, develop public speaking skills, engage in civic activism, and participate in community service. For nearly a decade, I have worked with and researched the CDF's Freedom School summer program, a summer program designed to support literacy, leadership development, and cultural pride among Black youth. My research explores how these alternative educational spaces serve as critical sites of empowerment for Black children and their families.

CDF Freedom Schools

In graduate school, I was exposed to the CDF's Freedom School Program. Several graduate students in my program worked in the summers with a couple of local universities that hosted the program. The program for me was life changing. My perspective had been as a previous teacher, I had not seen children as excited as these children were about learning.

The CDF Freedom School model is an approach to engage children in an integrated, culturally relevant literacy curriculum, implemented by college-aged Servant Leader Interns (SLIs). This was modeled after the Freedom Summer of 1964 in Mississippi. The role of a SLI is to serve as a role model by providing leadership and guidance to scholars from marginalized communities. By leveraging the experiences of college-educated youth, SLIs foster mentorship, academic support, and personal growth in the students they serve. The CDF FS model includes five essential components:

1. High-quality academic enrichment
2. Social action and civic engagement
3. Intergenerational servant leadership development
4. Nutrition, health, and mental health
5. Parent and family involvement (CDF Freedom Schools, 2025)

My colleague Allison LaGarry and I met in graduate school and worked together at Freedom School in the summer. Allison and I remained in touch with each other after our graduate school day and committed to working on researching Freedom Schools. This study involved two phases based on the *context* of caregiver engagement. At the beginning of our work, we administered Roadmap Family Engagement Survey (RFES) (Ishimaru & Lott, 2015) as a pre-test to determine caregivers' current engagement in and efficacy regarding school navigation. This survey asked parents how they felt about the schools they currently attend. Additionally, participants were given the option to participate in individual interviews. Individual interview participants received a Visa Gift Card for participating. All participants were informed of the purpose of the study, as well as their rights as participants, via a consent form (provided as part of the IRB application process).

The results of that survey indicated the following: 55 percent—Agreed they know special programs available at school or the district to help my child; 87.5 percent responded—I know how well my child is doing academically in school; 72 percent—I understand the steps my child needs to take in order to go to college; 73.08 percent—I know who to talk with at my school regarding my concerns or questions about my child's education; 47.37 percent—I know the community resources to help my child.

The results of the survey overwhelmingly indicated that they were aware of the programs and services available at their child's school. Parents demonstrated a strong awareness of the steps needed to prepare their child for college and had a clear understanding of their child's academic performance. However, where their knowledge was less extensive was in accessing community resources. This finding suggests that while parents can effectively navigate the academic aspects of their child's education, they face greater challenges in connecting with broader community support systems. This aligns with my previous research on mentoring programs, which indicates that parents often utilize these programs as a means of helping their child access essential community resources. The second phase of the study involved interviews, which revealed that the Freedom School program met many of the needs parents were seeking. The following key themes emerged from the interviews, highlighting the program's impact:

1. Preventing Summer Slide
2. Providing cultural enrichment
3. Opportunity to fill the gaps of school
4. Reinforcing the self-care in caregiving

CDF Freedom Schools is a holistic program designed to serve not only the scholars but also the SLIs and parents/caregivers. The primary focus of this program is to prevent summer slide through culturally relevant books that empower scholars to make a difference in their communities, nation, and world with hope, education, and action. One of the parents responded:

> What attracted me to it was a family member told me about it. I researched it, and I found out that it would have been a literacy program, to make sure that they didn't have regression over the summer. That means a lot to me, because trying to work, make sure they have somewhere safe to go over the summer, and make sure that they don't have any regression over the summer, where they're in a deficit when they start school, that means a lot to me.

This parent was deeply invested in their child's continued academic progress. Reinforcing findings from previous studies, it is evident that Black parents are highly engaged in their children's education. In fact, many actively seek out opportunities for learning and growth over the summer to ensure ongoing academic success.

With respect to providing cultural enrichment, a parent shared:

> What Freedom School means to me is there is something cultural for my child. Her going to a Black school, [that] was not really getting talked about . . . her culture. I just feel Freedom School just enhances what needs to be taught. Her being around more peers. Also, just having the experience of having her black teachers and stuff. She's never had a black teacher before.

The layers of cultural enrichment and reinforcement in the Freedom School programming are very intentional. The books used are culturally relevant and often not widely celebrated or centered in traditional classrooms that many students experience. Freedom School deliberately values and uplifts the lives of its students and families. This intention is reflected in the weekly book selections, where students—referred to as scholars—can see themselves in the characters and storylines. This act of representation is an essential anti-racist practice. As Professor Sims Bishop asserts, books should serve as "mirrors" for students, reflecting their identities and experiences (Perspectives, 1990). Children from marginalized communities must have the opportunity to see themselves in literature, just as all readers should be provided with windows that offer insights into diverse cultures and experiences.

When it comes to out-of-school opportunities, parents prioritize both mentoring and Freedom School programs as avenues for learning beyond what is emphasized in traditional school settings. In the context of mentoring, parents express a strong interest in social capital opportunities—specifically, ways to help their children navigate the challenges posed by structural racism, such as disproportionate discipline policies in schools. Additionally, many students in low-income and under-resourced schools face the reality of understaffed schools, further limiting their access to quality education. In North Carolina, this issue has been highlighted in the Leandro case. According to the Public School Forum of North Carolina:

> In 1994, five school districts in low-wealth counties along with families filed a lawsuit against the state (Leandro v. State of North Carolina) arguing that their school districts did not have enough money to provide an equal education for their children, despite the fact that they taxed their residents higher than average. Twenty-five years later, the Leandro case remains one of the biggest education policy issues in North Carolina—and those counties—Hoke, Halifax, Robeson, Vance, and Cumberland—which were among the lowest funded in the state, remain toward the bottom of our rankings in terms of their ability to support public schools on a per pupil basis. (*Leandro v. State of North Carolina*, Public School Forum, n.d.)

The lack of support and resources in public education forces parents to seek additional opportunities to supplement their child's learning. One parent shared:

> I feel like [public school] should be kind of a little different, but they say it's because that they don't have enough teachers, which is sad . . . . Then the classrooms get a little bigger and teachers can't handle it. And they always have a teacher straight from school . . . they don't last.

The sentiment this parent shared with me indicated their disappointment in classroom spaces that lacked the same joy and support that Freedom School provided. In this program, classrooms maintain a 1:10 ratio, fostering a more collaborative learning experience. This collaborative approach is woven throughout the program. Additionally, the intergenerational focus creates opportunities for parents and caregivers to learn from one another and connect with local community resources. Weekly meetings cover essential topics such as financial literacy, advocating for your child at school, understanding social emotional needs and self-care. One parent shared the following:

> How am I gonna tell them, "You can do anything you put your mind to, you can conquer any fear, any whatever, whether it's a fear, whether it's age, whether it's whatever?" But to have my babies sitting there, clapping for me, and rooting me on, and telling me I can do it, and to know I can't let my babies down. I can't do that. To think that my boy is up there drumming and doing it and not missing a beat. And I was like, "Okay, you gotta do it how you did when you did boy! You gotta do it!"

In this story, a mother shared that she decided to start swimming lessons after attending one of our self-care workshops. It was something she had always wanted to do but had a deep fear of swimming. Her motivation grew even stronger when, during one of our programs, her normally shy son participated in a drumming program. Watching him overcome his fear and perform in front of a large crowd inspired her to face her own fears. She reflected on how her children motivated her to keep going on her swim test day, pushing her to persist.

Her story reminds me of the power of Freedom School. This program demonstrates the need for out-of-school programs that validate the full humanity of children, especially in a society where Black and Brown children disproportionately are pushed out of their schools. They need to experience joy and laughter and have a space where intergenerational leadership and knowledge is appreciated.

Online Learning During the Pandemic: Families' Experiences and Hopes

Prior to the Covid-19 pandemic, the Freedom School program met weekly for tutoring. When the United States shut down we had to suspend our in-person meetings. As a parent of a newborn and a toddler, I was juggling childcare and work responsibilities. Given the challenges, I also wanted to learn more about how other families were navigating this new reality.

I assembled a research team, including Lily Parker, an undergraduate student, and Camry Wilborn Merer, a university employee in the Office of Civic and Community Engagement. With the help of the university communications team, we were able to get the study advertised on our local news outlets. With this support, we were able to generate widespread interest in our study. This outreach allowed us to hear from a diverse range of families who shared their experiences, frustrations, and wishes.

One mom shared that, between the four children in her family, they had to navigate over twenty platforms for school. Each child had different methods of communication with their teachers, and information was not streamlined. When we looked closer at the data, we saw that all of our respondents who were considered *essential workers or frontline workers* were Black or African American women. These mothers had varied experiences with online learning.

One mother described how her son, who attended a local charter school, did not have access to a computer and was given only worksheets to complete. Over time, his frustration grew, leading to the lack of participation. Another mother expressed appreciation for the small efforts of her child's teacher, such as sending small gifts and making home visits to keep morale up. She shared that, at times, they would meet their child's teacher at the school parking lot to access WIFI. However, not all families had the same experience. One mother shared that her work demands schedule prevented her from accessing the school district's WIFI hotspots, making it difficult for her child to complete online assignments.

The overall consensus among these families was a desire for open communication from educators. Many parents expressed frustration that they were not receiving ongoing updates about their child's learning. This mirrors concerns raised by parents in the mentoring program. In the online learning experience, some parents did not realize their child was struggling until grades were posted. One mother, nearly in tears, wished that someone—anyone—had simply called or sent a personal message to offer support.

Recommendations for Educators: Centering Black Families and Humanity

The examples above share a common thread: they provide spaces where students and families are seen, affirmed, and valued based on their strengths and humanity. In each case, parents and caregivers are highly engaged and actively seek opportunities to be involved. School-based mentoring programs are often designed to support marginalized students in their academic outcomes. However, to be truly effective, these programs must actively involve parents and caregivers, creating a holistic approach to student support. Additionally, it's crucial for non-Black mentors to understand the implications of racism and systemic oppression on their mentees' daily lives.

The CDF Freedom Schools, which began in 1995 as a reiteration of the Freedom Summer of 1964, exemplify the power of understanding the cultural and historical context of a community's fight for educational justice. The program embraces a multigenerational approach, fostering a love of learning and literacy while centering families in a human-centered, rather than deficit-based, model. This allows families and communities to thrive.

As we navigate a post Covid-19 world, school systems have recognized the importance of online platforms in maintaining continuity of instruction during disruptions like inclement weather.

However, another critical lesson from the shift to online learning is the essential role of clear and consistent communication with parents and caregivers. This is particularly true for marginalized families, where work schedules often lack flexibility. A parent or caregiver's demanding job does not mean that they do not care about their child's education—it often means they face structural barriers to engagement. As indicated in my own research, most of the mothers interviewed really appreciated the opportunity to be in open communication with their child's teacher. Schools and mentoring programs must continue fostering these connections to build stronger, more inclusive educational environments.

Drawing from these examples, I want to share actionable strategies for building relationships with families:

1. Empower Parents/Caregivers to Contribute Their Strengths

Allow parents and caregivers to engage in ways that align with their strengths. For example, if a parent excels in communication, invite them to lead a parent group that gathers and shares community resources with your organization.

2. Establish Consistent and Multiple Communication Channels

Research from my study on online learning during Covid-19 revealed that families wanted regular updates and diverse communication options. Utilize tools like ClassDojo to share pictures and messages, providing real-time insight into children's progress. Additionally, an online newsletter can keep families informed about upcoming events and engagement opportunities. Providing multiple communication avenues fosters a stronger sense of community.

3. Celebrate Families' Experiences and Cultural Knowledge

Go beyond traditional holidays—invite community experts who can share historical knowledge and cultural values. Identify local voices who can speak about significant historical figures, cultural traditions, or community legacies. In out-of-school programs, incorporate arts and sciences as tools to connect with and uplift cultural narratives.

4. Co-Design Programming with Families

Start each programming year with surveys and community conversations to learn how families envision the program supporting their needs. Identify local resources and collaborations that align with families' goals. Are there community members who can lead workshops? Small businesses that can provide catering? Organizations offering free student recognition resources? Creating these partnerships fosters sustainable, community-driven programming.

5. Train Volunteers and Staff in Anti-Racism and Equity

Ensure all staff and volunteers understand the complexities of racism and systemic oppression affecting students and their families. Provide training on how these inequities manifest in education, such as disproportionate discipline policies impacting Black, Latino, and Hispanic students. Encourage volunteers and staff to be vocal advocates for equity and create an environment where students feel supported and empowered.

Final Call to Action: Reframing How Educators View Black Families in Education

My mother-in-law passed away in August of 2024. It was one of the most painful experiences of my life. I loved her dearly—she was not only a great mother-in-law but also an incredible grandma. Her loss is felt by us daily. At her homegoing service, we set aside time for people to share their memories. We asked people to keep it short, three to four minutes at most. Person after person came forward, struggling to condense a lifetime of love, service, and advocacy into a few minutes.

For twenty years, my mother-in-law worked in Johnston and Wayne Counties of North Carolina working mostly for Boys and

Girls Clubs, where she served as director. Service was her life. She was constantly thinking about ways to support the kids in the community. In order to fully understand the magnitude of her service, you need to know something about the community in which she served.

Johnston County, North Carolina, has a long history of racial discrimination. Many locals recall it being known as a sundown town and home to active Ku Klux Klan presence. In an newspaper article titled "What's the History of Ku Klux Klan Billboards Near Smithfield? Curious NC Finds Out" published in the Raleigh News and Observer, the author outlines the history of Klan billboards on US Highway 70 (Cain, 2019). Though such billboards were scattered throughout the state, the ones in Johnston County were a stark reminder of the reality Black and Brown residents faced. Given this history, it's no surprise that educational and economic opportunities for Black youth in the county have remained limited. The formerly all-white high school is now predominantly Black, while white flight has created newer, more affluent schools in the area.

Amid these challenges, my mother-in-law was a fierce advocate for the kids she served—primarily Black and Brown youth from working-class backgrounds. During her service, former students shared stories of how she had shaped their lives. Many recalled memories of choir, drumming, college prep, and countless other experiences she provided. Parents and caregivers expressed their deepest gratitude for knowing their children would be loved and cared for, and they felt good leaving them under her care.

All of these expressions of gratitude matched the conversations she and I often had. In her last months on earth, she spoke passionately about her efforts to support her students. She shared how she had started a book club and a bowling club, tirelessly seeking community support to keep them running. She fundraised, secured in-kind donations, and ensured her students had access to experiences that enriched their lives.

She also shared her frustrations—particularly with colleagues who didn't believe in the children's potential and actively resisted her efforts. One such instance was a parent engagement event she organized. She envisioned an event that showered parents with appreciation, love, and excitement. Despite skepticism from colleagues who doubted parents would even show up, she personally invited families, engaging them with warmth and enthusiasm. She later described the night with excitement—how she had decorated, rolled out a red carpet for parents, and witnessed an overwhelming turnout. She had proven the doubters wrong.

In her last role, she opened a new club in an under-resourced area. She found a building that was only used in the mornings and convinced the owners to let her use it for an afterschool program and summer camp. She saw possibilities where others saw limitations. My mother-in-law was a true servant leader. She didn't hesitate to ask for resources for her "babies," as she called them. She advocated for them within the community and in their schools. If a child faced behavioral issues, she worked with school administrators to find solutions. Nothing deterred her from centering the humanity of the children and families she served. She listened, believed in, and fought for them. As we mourned her loss, now-adult former students shared how her unwavering belief in them had shaped their lives. Her advocacy, love, and persistence changed their trajectories.

As I close out this chapter, I urge you to center the humanity of the families and youth you work with, just as my mother-in-law did. No matter how others viewed the children she served, she knew their worth. She believed she could make a difference in their lives—and she did. She believed she could make a difference in their lives—and she did. Let her legacy be a reminder that every child is worth fighting for.

References

Cain, B. (2019, July 23). "What's the History of Ku Klux Klan Billboards Near Smithfield? CuriousNC Finds Out." *Raleigh News & Observer.* https://www.newsobserver.com/news/local/article232986152.html.

Children's Defense Fund. (2025, February 21). *CDF Freedom Schools®.* https://www.childrensdefense.org/our-work/cdf-freedom-schools/

de Souza Briggs, X. (1998). "Brown Kids in White Suburbs: Housing Mobility and the Many Faces of Social Capital." *Housing Policy Debate, 9*(1), 177–221. https://doi.org/xxxx.

Dominguez, S., and C. Watkins (2003). "Creating Networks for Survival and Mobility: Social Capital among African-American and Latin-American Low-income Mothers." *Social Problems, 50* (1), 111–35. https://doi.org/xxxx.

Du Bois, W. E. B. (2008). *The Souls of Black Folk* (B. H. Edwards, Ed.). Oxford University Press.

DuBois, D. L., and Karcher, M. J. (2005). "Youth mentoring." *Handbook of Youth Mentoring, 2*(11), 2–12.

Freedman, M. (1999). *The Kindness of Strangers: Adult Mentors, Urban Youth, and the New Voluntarism*. Cambridge University Press.

Hill Collins, P. (2009). *Black Feminist Thought: Knowledge, Consciousness, and the Politics of Empowerment* [2nd ed.]. Routledge.

Ishimaru, A., and J. Lott (2015). "Families in the Driver's Seat: Parent-driven Lessons and Guidelines for Collective Engagement." *The Equitable Parent–School Collaboration Research Project* (University of Washington), *The Road Map Project* (Community Center for Education Results), *Kent School District Parents, Teachers, Principals, and District Leaders*, and *The Bill & Melinda Gates Foundation*.

Keller, T. E. (2005). "A Systemic Model of the Youth Mentoring Intervention." *Journal of Primary Prevention, 26*(2), 169–188.

Landry, L. (2020, December 15). "What Is Human-centered Design?" *Harvard Business School Online Business Insights Blog*. https://online.hbs.edu/blog/post/what-is-human-centered-design.

Miller, A. (2007). "Best Practices for Formal Youth Mentoring." *The Blackwell Handbook of Mentoring: A Multiple Perspectives Approach*, 305–324.

Moll, L. C., C. Amanti, D. Neff, and N. González (1992). "Funds of Knowledge for Teaching: Using a Qualitative Approach to Connect Homes and Classrooms." *Theory into Practice, 31*(2), 132–41. https://doi.org/xxxx.

Moynihan, P. (1965). "The Negro Family: The Case for National Action." In R. Rainwater and W. Yancey (eds.), *The Moynihan Report and Politics of Controversy*, 47–132. MIT Press.

National Park Service. (2024, June 11). Quotations—Martin Luther King, Jr. Memorial. U.S. Department of the Interior. Retrieved August 25, 2025, from https://www.nps.gov/mlkm/learn/quotations.htm

Perspectives: Choosing and Using Books for the Classroom (1990). *Mirrors, Windows, and Sliding Glass Doors*. https://scenicregional.org/wp-content/uploads/2017/08/Mirrors-Windows-and-Sliding-Glass-Doors.pdf.

Public School Forum of North Carolina (n.d.). *Leandro v. State of North Carolina*. https://www.ncforum.org/leandro/.

Rong, X. L. (1996). "Effects of Race and Gender on Teachers' Perception of the Social Behavior of Elementary Students." *Urban Education, 31*(3), 261–90. https://doi.org/xxxx.

Spencer, R., Basualdo-Delmonico, A., and Lewis, T. O. (2011). "Working to Make It Work: The Role of Parents in the Youth Mentoring Process." *Journal of Community Psychology, 39*(1), 51–59.

Styles, M. B., and Morrow, K. V. (1992). *Understanding How Youth and Elders Form Relationships: A Study of Four Linking Lifetime Programs.* Public/Private Ventures, Philadelphia

Walker, G. (2005). "Youth Mentoring and Public Policy." In D. L. DuBois and M. J. Karcher (Eds.), *Handbook of Youth Mentoring* (pp. 510–524). Sage Publications Ltd. https://doi.org/10.4135/9781412976664.n3

Do not get lost in a sea of despair. Be hopeful, be optimistic. Our struggle is not the struggle of a day, a week, a month, or a year, it is the struggle of a lifetime. Never, ever be afraid to make some noise and get in good trouble, necessary trouble.

John Lewis—A tweet from June 2018

Introduction: The Call to Action

This chapter reminds readers of the work of those who come before us who fight for the long arch of equality. Though the fight is long, it is necessary for us to remain vigilant to move the needle. This chapter will outline the fight for justice in education, what those fights have yielded, and where they have left us to continue the work. This chapter reminds the reader that we cannot afford to separate ourselves as educators from those who fight and remain neutral and that what others before us have asked us to do is necessary. The framework from the previous chapter will be incorporated in this chapter. We will go back to some of those questions of thinking about whose story has been told and how teachers can do the work going forward.

In a tweet from John Lewis's personal Twitter account, he sent out the above quote in June 2018. This lifelong civil rights activist and elected politician served in the United States House of Representatives for Georgia's fifth congressional district from 1987 until his death in 2020. Mr. Lewis reminds us that the struggle for equality and human rights is a lifelong struggle. In 1963, Lewis was a speaker at the March on Washington for Jobs and Freedom. In his speech, he begins with:

> We march today for jobs and freedom, but we have nothing to be proud of. For hundreds and thousands of our brothers are not here. For they are receiving starvation wages, or no wages at all. While we stand here, there are sharecroppers in the Delta of Mississippi who are out in the fields working for less than three dollars a day, twelve hours a day. While we stand here there are students in jail on trumped-up charges. Our brother

> James Farmer, along with many others, is also in jail. We come here today with a great sense of misgiving. (Voices of Democracy, 2016)

Lewis goes on in the speech to describe the conditions which Black people are facing. In the same year following the march, Lewis became the chairman of the Student Nonviolent Coordinating Committee, also known as SNCC. This organization was an instrumental force in the Civil Rights Movement, particularly in the Southern states. Most notably, members of the SNCC organized lunch counter sit-ins and bus boycotts to bring awareness to the discrimination Black people were facing in Southern communities. Additionally, SNCC is known for their participation in Freedom Summer, a project to increase the number of registered Black voters and create educational programs for Black youth. In 2018, John Lewis tweeted, "Never, ever be afraid to make some noise and get in good trouble, necessary trouble," reflecting his lifelong commitment to advancing the rights and dignity of Black people.

Beginning in his early twenties and until his death at age eighty, Lewis continued the fight for justice. His leadership is a demonstration that the fight for justice isn't won overnight but rather is a collection of continuous actions that help improve outcomes over time. No one is coming to save us—it is up to ordinary people to fight for change, run for office, and organize collectively. In other words, neutrality is not an option. If we care about democracy and justice, regardless of race or economic status, we must commit to being organizers and activists who strengthen our communities. By doing so, we protect the investments that serve children, their families, and society as a whole.

As you read this chapter, you will learn how ordinary people throughout history chose to engage in 'good trouble' to create meaningful change. That history of organizing highlights the power we have in the present to stand in solidarity with school boards across the country and participate in the fight against Trump's efforts to dismantle public education. Additionally, this chapter emphasizes that being an anti-racist educator involves not only directly supporting students and their families but also critically examining educational systems and their underlying government structures. It stresses that the decisions that are being made in Washington, D.C. influence what happens at the state and local levels. Educators' understanding of how these broader decisions impact the classroom and how we can impact those decisions is another important step in driving systematic transformation.

The Legacy of the Fight for Justice in Education

In January 2025, the Trump administration pledged to close the US Department of Education, as it contends it is a place of wasteful government spending. However, what is missing from that argument is an understanding of what the Department of Education does. According to the US Department of Education website, the original organization opened in 1867 to help states establish school systems. Over the years, the duties of the department transformed and grew exponentially in the 1960s and 1970s:

> The anti-poverty and civil rights laws of the 1960s and 1970s brought about a dramatic emergence of the Department's equal access mission. The passage of laws such as Title VI of the Civil Rights Act of 1964, Title IX of the Education Amendments of 1972, and Section 504 of the Rehabilitation Act of 1973 which prohibited discrimination based on race, sex, and disability, respectively made civil rights enforcement a fundamental and long-lasting focus of the Department of Education. In 1965, the Elementary and Secondary Education Act launched a comprehensive set of programs, including the Title I program of Federal aid to disadvantaged children to address the problems of poor urban and rural areas. And in that same year, the Higher Education Act authorized assistance for postsecondary education, including financial aid programs for needy college students. (U.S. Department of Education, 2024)

While this administration begins to attempt to undo the rights of students across the country, the most vulnerable will be those for whom this office has had the oversight of protecting, which include students of color, students in rural communities, low-income students, students with exceptionalities, and students from the LGBTQ community.

Although communities are fighting to protect the department and the interest of their communities in the contemporary world, this struggle is not new. Activism, especially around racial justice, has been a continued fight in American educational spaces for decades.

Historical Struggles for Educational Justice

The year 2024 marked the seventieth anniversary of *Brown v. Board of Education* (1954). This landmark case was pivotal in the integration of Black and Brown students into primarily white schools. An unanticipated outcome from *Brown v. Board of Education* included the delaying of school districts to follow the law. In some cases, school districts decided to close rather than integrate. Additionally, Black teachers were let go at unprecedented rates; if they were allowed to stay, they did not receive the same rate of compensation. According to a report from Wesson (2024), the timeline for desegregation litigation continued well into the 1990s. A few to note are the following:

- 1969: In the *Alexander v. Holmes County (MS) Board of Education* decision, the US Supreme Court ruled that school districts were obligated to eliminate racial segregation "at once" rather than "at all deliberate speed," which had allowed school districts to stall in the implementation of the goals of the Brown decision. The Supreme Court declared that the all deliberate speed standard is no longer constitutionally permissible, and the court ordered an immediate desegregation of Mississippi schools. (Wesson, 2024)

- 1971: In the *Swann v. Charlotte Mecklenburg Board of Education* decision, the US Supreme Court upheld using busing as a means of integrating public school systems. The decision furnished school districts with an effective tool for desegregating schools where students had previously been racially isolated. The strategy typically called for the busing of students of color to all-white schools and busing white students to schools with enrollments of predominantly students of color. Although it was considered a controversial strategy by some, busing frequently achieved the desired desegregation goals. The court also approved magnet schools, compensatory education, and other tools as remedies to counterbalance residential segregation, which remained a major obstacle to school integration. (Wesson, 2024)

- 1988: School integration in the United States reached its all-time high. Almost 45 percent of the nation's Black students were enrolled in majority-white schools. After this point, a downward trajectory began. (Wesson, 2024)
- 1993: The US Supreme Court ruled that a school district with boundaries drawn in "bizarre" (gerrymandered) configurations for no other visible reason other than to segregate certain racial or ethnic groups is an unconstitutional practice. (Wesson, 2024)

What we have learned from these past struggles is that there was not a clear strategy for integration following the litigation. We have seen over the years that instead of integration, we have seen an increase in *Defacto Segregation,* which is a Latin word for "by fact." While the law stated that schools must integrate, segregation remains prevalent in certain areas due to factors like neighborhood demographics and the availability of private and homeschooling options. Additionally, amid the process of the pursuit of educational justice, there has been a recognition of what practices and pedagogies best suit Black and Brown students. Although the road has been far from linear, there are wins and there are losses, the fight for anti-racism, especially in the context of schooling, has been and continues to be led by those who are dedicated to making schools and communities better. Scholars often believe that if Black communities were able to be fully funded, the outcomes would have been better than where we are today. Dr. Gloria Ladson-Billings (2024) asserts

> I asked, "Can we at least have Plessy?" I was suggesting that if was better to have a "real Plessy" than a "fake Brown." A real Plessy would mean that the separate schools Black and Brown children find themselves in

would be required to have equitable funding, equally qualified teachers, and equal curricular materials as their White middle-income peers. I argued that it was clear that school districts were not going to ever truly desegregate and since Black and Brown children were going to remain in segregated enclaves, why can't we do right by them in their own communities? (p. 13)

The challenge of educating Black and Brown students in public schools that utilize federal funding has been a continued push and pull to obtain equal opportunities and treatments to those of white students. Various organizations and citizens have worked to ensure that those protections are rightly granted.

The Danger of Neutrality

In an era where racism, anti-immigration, and homophobia are increasingly vocal and prevalent on social media, remaining neutral is more harmful than one may think. Neutrality leaves room to be on either side of an issue. Many educators will hint at things like, I'm not political––some educators don't see themselves as activists. However, I assert that remaining neutral, especially on issues of racism and anti-immigration, poses a serious danger to our most vulnerable students. As an anti-racist educator, taking action is a part of the equation. In fact, the commitment to action must be a lifelong commitment. It requires a commitment to learning and unlearning, reading the past, and reading for the future. It requires a willingness to speak up and out against injustice. It requires a calling out of those who commit harms. I often tell my students that in education they should also consider themselves in the same vein as a healthcare professional; being of service to their students is also a life-or-death matter. The seriousness of being an anti-racist educator is also in conjunction with the idea of serving all your students with a holistic approach. Recognizing how a student's identity is shaped by their families, their communities, and their cultures is a moral and ethical duty of all educators. Given that each facet of these identities cannot be separated, it is important that when policies and practices alienate students based on race, educators must not remain neutral.

Engaging in Activism as an Educator

When I reflect on my activism as an educator, I think of my decade-long role with CDF Freedom Schools. CDF Freedom Schools® offer summer and afterschool enrichment through a research-based, multicultural model that supports K-12 scholars and their families. The program emphasizes academic and character development, family involvement, civic engagement, intergenerational leadership, and holistic well-being. The program is modeled after Freedom Summer of 1964, a summer that aimed to mobilize Black citizens in Mississippi to be able to vote and be educated with the support of college students from the north. This Civil Rights Movement effort was organized by Bob Moses of the SNCC. In 2013, I began my journey as a SLI at Duke University's Freedom School, in Durham, North Carolina, intentionally looking for a summer job. After the summer, I came to understand the importance of activism as an educator, which has driven me to continue in the tradition of Marian Wright Edelman, founder of the CDF, an organization dedicated to advocating for children. The organization has taught me what servant leadership is and what it means to be an anti-racist educator. The founder of CDF, Mrs. Marian Wright Edelman, in a 2012 speech outlines servant leadership as a way of leading that prioritizes the needs and well-being of others, especially children and marginalized communities, above personal gain or ambition. She emphasizes that true leadership is about standing up for what is right, even when it's difficult, and working tirelessly to create a better future for all (Children's Defense Fund, 2012).

Mrs. Edelman, the first Black woman to pass the bar exam in Mississippi, continued the fight for justice by continuing the effort of the original Freedom Schools from 1964. In 1995, she established two Freedom Schools with her organization, the CDF. Since then, CDF, in partnership with schools, colleges, universities, churches, and community centers across the country, has served over 200,000 children who have attended Freedom School and over 20,000 young people—the SLIs who work as camp teachers have been trained in the curriculum and pedagogy of the historic program. Professor Jon Hale recently wrote for Time Magazine online the need for Freedom School sixty years after the original project. Hale states:

> Today, the Freedom Schools continue to instill lessons of the past and for democracy. Freedom Schools will continue to assign books that center the experiences of children and families historically marginalized. Moreover, the Children's Defense Fund each year designates a day of "social action" to work with students to address areas of inequality. (Hale, 2024)

Through the Freedom School movement, we can serve children and families in their whole humanity. We can work with communities and school systems that recognize the power of joy and the power of allowing children to find joy through literacy. In doing so, we move beyond narratives that aim to paint a picture that Black families are not involved or that children cannot learn. We are doing this by having a place where parents show up, eat meals, participate in morning meetings, go on field trips, and donate supplies and snacks. The simple ways of being involved allow for a human connection and a place for families to be connected make Freedom School special. By pushing to move beyond the narrative that we know only aims to denigrate us, we work in community to uplift and center justice, joy, and humanity. It has not always been easy finding resources, moving around challenging situations, or just plain moving past the haters, but it's necessary work.

In tough times, you must find what drives you to support Black and Brown families, even when the challenges seem insurmountable. This advocacy can take many forms—speaking up in a school or community program, serving on a school board, county commission, city council, or even as mayor to champion Black and Brown educational needs. It might also mean joining a national advocacy organization. Wherever your advocacy leads you, these efforts are crucial in ensuring that policies, curricula, and community engagement push leaders and institutions to be actively anti-racist and empathetic. Do this work in community, for within community, you can rely on each other and mobilize toward a better future.

Bringing the Framework to Life: Reexamining Our Role

In the previous chapter, I outlined thinking about whose story is being told and who benefits from those stories and systems. In this moment of the Trump administration, in the first sixty days of this term, the Federal Government has acted with alarming speed to eliminate critical funding for educational programs—particularly those designed to support and uplift diverse communities through equity and inclusion. When we engage in this work, we must remember that centering humanity is not a bad thing. Rather, centering perspectives and communities allows us to understand and embrace the lived experiences of all communities, ensuring our advocacy is targeting the needs and desires of the people.

Implementing Actionable Change

Remember, John Lewis reminds us not to get lost in despair. Since the new federal administration took office in 2025, I have observed countless social media posts and news reports on what their policies will be going forward. For myself, as an educator who works in a number of these spaces that the policies are aimed at, many of the communities I work with have sent out widespread messages addressing how these policies will affect the organization moving forward. For example, the US Department of Education put out a letter on February 14, 2025, which has become known as the *Dear Colleague Letter*. School systems, colleges, and universities received this letter outlining how the last several years have been discriminatory toward, in a way that was detrimental to what was implied, white students. The letter outlines the Supreme Court's 2023 decision in *Students for Fair Admissions v. Harvard* (SFFA), which clarified that the use of racial preferences in college admissions is unlawful. The letter goes further by saying:

> Other programs discriminate in less direct, but equally insidious, ways. DEI programs, for example, frequently preference certain racial groups and teach students that certain racial groups bear unique moral burdens that others do not. Such programs stigmatize students who belong to particular racial groups based on crude racial stereotypes. Consequently, they deny students the ability to participate fully in the life of a school. (Trainor, 2025)

The argument that these programs stigmatize white students at schools is a gross misinterpretation of what these programs aim to do. For example, Winston Salem Teach, a program I have worked with, aims to get people qualified to work in Title 1 schools. This program is in a partnership with three universities: Winston Salem State University, Salem College, and Wake Forest University. Students in this program are being prepared to work in the areas of special education, elementary education, and secondary education. This collaborative program is a recipient of a grant from the US Department of Education. This program allows its students to participate in four years of intentional professional development, all while earning a living income. This program was established to help a significant need in the community.

Strategies for Integrating Justice-Oriented Teaching in Daily Practice

Recently, mobilization strategies have focused on calling state and national elected officials to emphasize the importance of these programs. Additionally, people have come together to vocalize what the program means to raise awareness around the program. In doing so, additional funding sources have been secured.

Find ways to partner with local organizations that support the mission of uplifting Black and Brown communities in anti-racist ways. For example, partnering with Black-led nonprofits that aim to bring awareness to issues faced by Black youth is another way I have found community in student advocacy. Action4Equity is one that stands out. According to their website, they are:

> We are a Black-led, intentionally multi-racial coalition of parent and family leaders, activists and accomplices, moral obligators, and philanthropists building a movement to achieve justice through an educational equity policy framework. (About Us Action4Equity, 2023)

By working with the coalition of intentional communities, we are able to advocate for what parents would like to see in their children's educational outcomes. Leveraging my research background, I collaborated with parents to implement participatory action research (PAR) methods, empowering them as key drivers of data collection and analysis. In a particular study, we focused on exploring questions related to pre-K education and the development of culturally affirming environments that support young children's learning and identity development. Through a collaborative partnership involving a local community agency, Black parents, and a university researcher, the project emphasized capacity building and community-driven inquiry. Participants engaged in a comprehensive learning process, where they developed foundational knowledge of qualitative research, designed research questions grounded in their lived experiences, and conducted rigorous data collection.

The parent researchers were a group of local parents with no formal academic titles or training. They were involved parents who collectively wanted to see a change in the way schools interacted with their Black children. The parents involved in this project worked with the local nonprofit to find ways to support their community to find solutions to lead to a pre-k system that valued them as families. I trained the parents to collect data through interviews, focus groups, and observations, enabling them to provide rich insights into the ways culturally affirming practices can enhance early childhood education. These efforts not only elevated their voices in educational research but also equipped them to advocate for systemic changes that directly address community needs. The findings from this project highlighted the critical role of family engagement in shaping equitable educational practices for

Black and Brown students. This type of partnership allows for Black parents' voices to emerge as experts, thus leading to advocacy in the community as it relates to pre-K opportunities. In communities with researchers who can support PAR methods, this advocacy approach can highlight key areas that benefit from research-driven insights, helping inform policymakers about community needs. In this example, the research has been presented nationally, allowing others to replicate the model in their own communities.

Furthermore, daily advocacy can be creating a space that highlights and uplifts the voices of students. Is there artwork on the wall? Are there books featuring students that come from the same background as your students and those in the community? Can you find ways to allow parents/caregivers to have access to your space? Having them volunteer? Can they lead a lesson on something from their culture that aligns with what you are teaching? Are you in community with Black and Brown-led nonprofit organizations and community organizations that you can learn from? Many of these organizations will host gatherings and speakers to provide support around topics such as parent engagement, pedagogy, and advocacy aimed at the community.

Another way to stay justice-centered is to join national organizations that aim to dismantle racism and provide educators the opportunity to further grow. Below are some to consider:

- We Are, working to extend anti-racist education (https://www.weare-nc.org/): We Are is a Durham, North Carolina-based 501(c)(3) dedicated to anti-racist education through summer camps for children, professional development for educators, and workshops for families. In February 2023, Executive Director Ronda Taylor Bullock was honored at the Vice President's house as an emerging Black leader during Black History Month. (Durham Non-Profit Leader Recognized as Emerging Black Leader in Country, 2023)

- Racial Equity Institute (REI): The REI in Greensboro, North Carolina, offers workshops and training to help individuals and organizations address structural racism. In 2016, Ben & Jerry's staff traveled to North Carolina to learn from REI about racial equity. REI equips communities with tools to challenge power structures and build equitable systems. (The Racial Equity Institute, 2025)

- African American Policy Forum (AAPF): The AAPF, led by Executive Director and co-founder Kimberlé Crenshaw, is a think tank dedicated to dismantling structural inequality. AAPF connects academics, activists, and policymakers to promote racial and gender justice through intersectional frameworks and policy transformation. (Intersectionality, 2025)

- Learning for Justice: A Program of the Southern Poverty Law Center: Learning for Justice promotes racial justice by providing educational resources to dismantle white supremacy and strengthen inclusive democracy. It offers lesson plans, toolkits, films, and more to support civic and political education for all. Learning for justice. (2025)

- Equal Justice Initiative (EJI): The EJI, founded by Bryan Stevenson in 1989, works to end mass incarceration, challenge racial and economic injustice, and protect human rights. EJI provides legal services to those unfairly convicted and operates the Legacy Museum and National Memorial for Peace and Justice. Engaging with organizations like EJI supports ongoing learning and community-led anti-racism efforts. https://eji.org/ (Equal Justice Initiative, 2025)

In these examples, you can find ways to stay connected to organizations that promote learning about ways to dismantle racism and ways to continue your journey in anti-racism practices. These resources offer materials that can be used in educational spaces and help develop you as an educator. As with all community work, it is also important to seek out community-led initiatives and organizations that are committed to anti-racism efforts in your local community.

Sustaining the Fight: Moving Forward with Hope

Through my work with parents in the PAR project, I've learned that hope drives their vision of what is possible. This hope is the foundation of what Black parents believe can be achieved. In this case, it fuels the nonprofit, the community, and the parents to advocate for policies and practices that center the humanity of Black and Brown students. Without this hope, there can be no vision for a better future.

Overcoming Burnout and Resistance

Remember the path to liberation is long. You must be in community with others who are like-minded and can help you remember you are a part of a collective. This work cannot be sustained when people work individually. According to a 2022 Gallup survey:

> 44% (of K-12 workers) say they "always" or "very often" feel burned out at work, outpacing all other industries nationally. College and university workers have the next-highest burnout level, at 35%, making educators among the most burned out groups in the U.S. workforce. (Marken and Agrawal, 2022)

The emotional toll of balancing the demands of working in educational settings with anti-racist activism can create an environment ripe for burnout. Prioritizing mindfulness is essential in sustaining this work. It is important to find joy in your daily routines. It is also important to know that the work you are doing might not be for everyone, and trying to convince people who are not interested in learning more or growing is not worth your time. There are plenty of people who can come along for the ride and want to learn more. We get to decide who and where we want to spend our time. There will be times where we will need to put our heads together and decide what will be the best ways to support our Black and Brown students. *What will be the best way we can show up for them in meaningful anti-racist ways?* There will be days when not everyone will understand or try to understand, and that will be okay. Thus, while you are on the journey of doing anti-racist work, it will be important for you to refuel, find joy, and center your mental, emotional, and physical health.

The Power of Collective Action

The power of the collective will make the journey toward anti-racist practices more sustainable. This means being in community not only with educational professionals, but also with students, families, and community members. There is a humanity that is built in the everyday: sharing meals, participating in extracurricular activities, and attending community events are all ways that allow for humanness and building relationships. Learning more about others gives you less room to have the mentality of *them versus me*. The narrative of *them* takes away the capacity to see how *they* are like the many people I've outlined here—just people who want the very best for their children. They want the best education to be accessible for their students and they want to be able to support them in any way they can; they attempt to work around system racism to continue to push to make their child's experience the best it can be.

Conclusion: The Urgency of Now

The fight for justice is ongoing and necessary, even more in times of crisis. In this particular moment in time, we are experiencing several competing efforts around public education, banned books, and the anti-DEI movement. The movement for humanity-centered educational spaces is critical. Committing to *Good Trouble* is the way forward to making our classrooms, communities, and youth centers a place where we all can thrive. This fight is a lifelong commitment, and we dedicate ourselves to making the next generation better.

References

Action4Equity. (2023, June 2). *About Us*. https://www.action4equityws.org/about-us/.

African American Policy Forum, United States. (2025). *Intersectionality*. https://www.aapf.org/.

Children's Defense Fund. (2012, February 15). *Marian Wright Edelman on the Need for Student Leadership Now* [Video]. YouTube. https://www.youtube.com/watch?v=8KhD38trKko.

Durham non-profit leader recognized as emerging Black leader in country. (2023, March 9). *ABC11 Raleigh-Durham*. https://abc11.com/durham-educator-black-leader-recognized-on-national-level/12931756/.

Equal Justice Initiative. (2025, March 6). *Equal Justice Initiative*. https://eji.org.

Hale, J. (2024, July 8). "60 Years Later, Freedom Schools Are Still Radical—and Necessary." *TIME*. https://time.com/6992744/freedom-schools-history/.

Ladson-Billings, G. (2024). *But What About the Teachers? The Forgotten Narratives of Black Teachers in the Midst of Brown.* Spencer Foundation, Learning Policy Institute, California Association of African-American Superintendents and Administrators.

Learning for Justice. (2025). *Learning for Justice*. https://www.learningforjustice.org.

Marken, S., and S. Agrawal (2022, June 13). *K-12 Workers Have Highest Burnout Rate in U.S.* Gallup. https://news.gallup.com/poll/393500/workers-highest-burnout-rate.aspx.

The Racial Equity Institute. (2025, January 28). *Movement Minded | Racial Equity Institute | Developing Tools*. Racial Equity Institute. https://racialequityinstitute.org/.

Trainor, C. (2025). *United States Department of Education Office for Civil Rights the Acting Assistant Secretary*. https://www.ed.gov/media/document/dear-colleague-letter-sffa-v-harvard-109506.pdf.

U.S. Department of Education. (2024, May 23). *Federal Role in Education*. U.S. Department of Education. https://www.ed.gov/about/ed-overview/federal-role-in-education.

Voices of Democracy. (2016, July 5). *Lewis, 'Speech at the March on Washington,' Speech Text—Voices of Democracy*. https://voicesofdemocracy.umd.edu/lewis-speech-at-the-march-on-washington-speech-text/.

Wesson, K. A. (2024). *A Timeline of the African-American Struggle for Desegregation and Equity Prior to and Since the Brown v. Board of Education Decision.* Spencer Foundation, Learning Policy Institute, California Association of African-American Superintendents and Administrators.

About the Author

Dani Parker Moore is a scholar, educator, and researcher specializing in parent engagement and community-based education. As the founder and director of the Wake Forest University Freedom School, she brings extensive expertise in working with families, educators, and communities to advance equity in education.